MW01528073

You Can't Take It With You ...
So How Will You Leave It Behind?

needs a space ☺

A "Plain English" Guide to Wills and Trusts

by
Steven W. Allen, JD

also, we always used a comma before the "and" in a series of items, etc.

this ";" is important for meaning

Copyright © 2007, Legal Awareness Series, LLC.

All rights reserved. The text of this publication, or any part thereof, may not be reproduced in any manner whatsoever without written permission from the publisher. No parts of this book may be used or reproduced except in accordance with the instructions contained within its pages. Each person's estate has unique and potentially complex legal, business, and tax issues. Your failure to properly consider such issues, or your misuse of the contents of these pages, could result in significant adverse consequences to you, your estate and the estate plan you are trying to establish. Of necessity, therefore, neither the author nor the publisher can give any assurances regarding the end result of your use of this information. You alone are responsible for the consequences of the use of this information and for making proper legal, tax, and business decisions. "This publication is designed to provide accurate and authoritative information in regard to the subject matter covered. It is sold with the understanding that the publisher is not engaged in rendering legal, accounting, or other professional service. If legal advice or other expert assistance is required, the services of a competent professional person should be sought."—From a Declaration of Principles jointly adapted by a Committee of the American Bar Association and Committee of Publishers and Associations.

Legal Awareness Series, Inc. "You Can't Take It With You ... So How Will You Leave It Behind?" *space / only one space*

ISBN 978-1-8790339-7-9

About the Author

Steven W. Allen, JD, expert estate planning attorney, has practiced law for over 30 years. His specialty is wills and trusts. Steven has helped thousands of people like you properly set up their personal estate plans to protect their assets, minimize taxes, and preserve family relationships. He works with clients individually and speaks to groups throughout the United States about estate planning. Visit his website at *www.StevenAllen.com* or *www.EstatePlanningDr.com* for information and to subscribe to his electronic newsletter, *Secrets of Wealth Preservation.*

[handwritten annotation, top left diagonal: "I think it would be more pleasing to the eye if the names of the authors all started at a consistent point on the page."]

Testimonials

"If you want to take care of the people you love, this book is a must-read. Steven has a unique way of making complex legal topics easy to understand. Finally, an attorney who speaks English! If you want to protect yourself, if you want to protect your assets, and if you want to leave a legacy for your family, this book will give you sound advice on how to do that."

—BARBARA J. BRUNO, CPC
PRESIDENT, HR SEARCH, INC.
GOOD AS GOLD TRAINING

[handwritten annotation: "I would put only the testimony givers name and 'letters' on the first line." (A)]

"The topic of death and trusts isn't comfortable but is unavoidable. When it comes to knowing this subject, I have yet to encounter anyone better than Steven Allen. His book is clear and amazing. Clearly, there is never a better time to address this topic than now. Read this, make some decisions, and get started!"

—PETER R. HOLYK, MD, CNS
FOUNDER OF CONTEMPORARY HEALTH INNOVATIONS

"Good Advice from a great lawyer, presented in a way anyone can understand. Get it."

—RANDY GAGE, AUTHOR, "WHY YOU'RE DUMB, SICK AND BROKE …AND HOW TO GET SMART, HEALTHY AND RICH!"

[handwritten annotation: "space"]

"Steve's book is an easy-to-read guide to estate planning … and more. He expertly uses real-life examples to explain living trusts. His convincing arguments will press you into action. You must create a living trust NOW to fully protect your family. I know Steve and trust his wisdom. I'm thankful he has shared his expertise with us."

—BETH TERRY, CSP, SPEAKER,
AUTHOR OF "101 WAYS TO MAKE YOUR LIFE EASIER"

[handwritten annotation at bottom: "(A) Any of these rest of his/her qualifications should start the same right to left point."]

"If you want to build your estate plan, know why and how, and be entertained along the way, read "You Can't Take It With You ... So How Will You Leave It Behind?" Nothing compares to Steve's clear explanation. He makes it easy to understand. Steve even has a great name—and we're not even related."

—DEBBIE ALLEN, AUTHOR, INTERNATIONAL BUSINESS SPEAKER
AND AWARD WINNING AUTHOR OF "CONFESSIONS OF
SHAMELESS SELF PROMOTERS" AND "SKYROCKETING SALES"

"With easy-to-understand language, clarity and wit, Steve carries his convincing message about using a trust as the foundation of estate planning. Everyone should read this book!"

—NAOMI R. RHODE, CSP, CPAE, SPEAKER HALL OF FAME,
CAVETT AWARD RECIPIENT, PAST NATIONAL PRESIDENT OF NATIONAL
SPEAKERS ASSOCIATION AND INTERNATIONAL FEDERATION FOR
PROFESSIONAL SPEAKERS, AND CO-FOUNDER OF SMART HEALTH

"This book will potentially save you thousands of dollars when life's ultimate assurance happens ... upon your death and distribution of your hard earned riches. But during your life ... it may bring you peace and comfort knowing that your loved ones will in fact receive your worldly goods in the manner in which YOU choose for them. This book may also save your emotional health and sanity ..."

—TED ROGERS, CREATOR OF "THE 10% FACTOR, WINNING IN THE WORLD
TODAY," PAST PRESIDENT OF THE ARIZONA CHAPTER OF THE
NATIONAL SPEAKERS ASSOCIATION, AND KNOWN AS "AMERICA'S PEAK
PERFORMANCE EXPERT," FOUNDER OF INSPIRED LIVING SYSTEMS

"In my Book "The Millionaire Maker," I advise my readers to use a living trust. I urge you to read Steve's book to learn why creating a trust is critical for you and your family. If you're building wealth, you must have a trust."

—LORAL LANGEMEIER, SPEAKER, AUTHOR OF "THE MILLIONAIRE MAKER:
ACT, THINK, AND MAKE MONEY THE WAY THE WEALTHY DO" AND "THE
MILLIONAIRE MAKER'S GUIDE TO WEALTH CYCLE INVESTING"

"*You Can't Take It With You* is a winner. I enjoyed its easy-to-read format. From cover to cover it is loaded with valuable practical information. Your action items, tips and links to website information are pure gold. Your book is the first I have seen to successfully explain, in plain English, the advantage of using trusts. Well written and essential reading for everyone."

—EDWARD OLKOVICH, EDWARD OLKOVICH LAW PROFESSIONAL CORPORATION, CERTIFIED SPECIALIST (ESTATES AND TRUST LAW)

"Steve Allen's estate planning strategies will save your family money and heartache. I should know because he handled my Family Trust and his book, *You Can't Take It With You* inspired me take action now. Get the book. Read it. And you'll soon find out if you've overlooked any of the important details to avoid probate and taxes."

—ALEX MANDOSSIAN, ELECTRONIC MARKETING STRATEGIST AND CEO OF HERITAGE HOUSE PUBLISHING, INC

And about Steve's presentations . . .

"I have been a member of the bars of Virginia, New York, and Arizona for over half a century, and I say without reservation your presentation was the finest I have ever heard explaining the great savings that can be made by proper estate planning. Not only was your presentation clear and instructive, but you are gifted with a sense of humor which made the entire presentation enjoyable."

—CAVETT ROBERT; LAWYER, SPEAKER, AUTHOR, FOUNDER OF THE NATIONAL SPEAKERS ASSOCIATION

Dedication

To my many clients who have shared
these experiences with me over the years.

Acknowledgments

A book is never the effort of one person. In this case, an entire team was involved. I want to thank my editors, Rosemary Green and Barbara McNichol, as well as my dutiful and dependable staff, Kari VanNoy, Juli Walsh and Melinda Sandberg. I also want to thank everyone who contributed passages to this book, or who were involved in cases, situations and anecdotes—either anonymously or posthumously. And, of course, special thanks to my wife and sweetheart, Linda, for her constant encouragement, assistance, and love, and for shepherding this book to completion.

great

Sentent

*How can you know for sure
if you don't even try?*

Table of Contents

Prologue: Why Read This Book?..................... 13

Introduction: Plan Your Estate Now................. 15

Chapter One: The Lowdown on Wills 19

Chapter Two: The Probate Factor.................... 31

Chapter Three: Trusts versus Wills.................. 43

Chapter Four: "Trust Me... "....................... 65

Chapter Five: Twelve Costly Misconceptions......... 103

Chapter Six: Questions About Trusts 115

Chapter Seven: It's Time to "Just Do It!" 139

Chapter Eight: Keeping Your Assets Safe from Lawsuits,
Creditors, and Judgments 151

Chapter Nine: What If You're Not Rich but Still Want
Protection? 195

Chapter Ten: "If I Own a Business, How Can I Protect
My Assets from Creditors, Predators, and Probate?".. 203

Chapter Eleven: Track Your Business Deductions and
Give Yourself a Raise 219

Chapter Twelve: How to Link Your Business Entities
to Your Estate Plan........................... 231

Chapter Thirteen: Something for Doctors to Consider.. 237

Chapter Fourteen: Special Suggestions for Multi-level
Marketers 243

Chapter Fifteen: Your Estate Planning Action List 247

Index 257

Prologue: Why Read This Book?

I just finished editing this book—and I'm Angry. Yup, that's Angry with a capital *A*. Why am I Angry? While reviewing it, I experienced one of the most distressing "if only" thoughts of my life. If only I'd known the simple truths contained in this book before my parents passed away! This book could have saved me—and six of my siblings—unbelievable emotional suffering. And cold, hard, cash to boot!

It's tragic that the average person takes more time to plan the family vacation than to plan the family's future. Plus, it's unfortunate that your estate plan—or lack of it—may become how you're remembered by your loved ones. In the event of your death, dealing with your estate is much easier for your family if you have a fully completed living trust. Lack of estate planning is a disaster waiting to happen. Tragically, that disaster can happen to the people you care most about. Even those who have prepared a traditional will can, upon their death, thrust a huge mess into the lives of their loved ones.

Please read on. Within these eye-opening pages you'll find what I found: The simple answer to what my parents should have done to prevent a horrible ordeal for their children and grandchildren. Learn how this simple answer can help you and your family. It's worth the read!

Most sincerely,

Rosemary Green

Introduction: Plan Your Estate Now

It can be painful to look back at certain decisions you made in life and see where you could've done better. For an attorney, that experience can be especially painful. In fact, I wish I could change one piece of advice I gave to a client many years ago whose heirs would have by far benefited greatly if I'd given her different advice. (You'll find the story in Chapter Three.)

I can't turn back the clock, but I've learned much through my 30 years of practicing estate planning. I'm excited to share the many money-saving, time-saving, hassle-saving, and relationship-saving tips I've learned during the past three decades.

The concept for this book was sparked when a friend of mine, a lawyer, expressed surprisingly incorrect views about trusts—a fundamental tool in the estate planning toolkit. I've been practicing law in the Phoenix, Arizona, area since 1973. My specialty is wills and trusts. I work with individual clients, plus I travel extensively speaking to groups across the country about the problems and challenges of estate planning. As I thought more about it, that spark exploded into a roaring blaze! My eyes opened to the dramatic need for this book: an easy-to-understand guide to help you plan your estate *now* and save money, time, hassle, and even relationships in the future.

I sincerely want to help you enjoy your property during your lifetime—after all, it's yours! And I want you to be able to pass the unused portion of your estate—with the least possible loss in value—to your loved ones. It's fair and just to do so. But sadly, that seldom happens. Unfortunately, I've observed many tragic situations in which people had put off their estate planning until it was too late, causing anguish among family members and friends.

Over the years, I've amassed pertinent information about estate planning with this goal: maximize the protection of assets while minimizing taxes. Plus, I've learned a few things about human nature and how people react when faced with the seemingly overwhelming prospect of estate planning. Therefore, I've distilled my knowledge and experience into this book of easy-to-understand tips, definitions, and advice. I promise that you won't feel overwhelmed. Armed with this book, you can now plan your estate for you—and yours!

—Steven W. Allen, JD
September 2006

What is Estate Planning?

My favorite description of estate planning is the National Network of Estate Planning Attorneys' definition:

"I want to control my property while alive, take care of my loved ones and myself if I become disabled, and, upon my death, give what I have to whom I want, the way I want, and when I want. And if I can, I want to save every last tax dollar, professional fee, and court cost possible."

Chapter One

The Lowdown on Wills

You might be surprised to discover that you don't have to be a John D. Rockefeller or Bill Gates to have an estate. Everyone has an estate. *Merriam-Webster's Dictionary* defines an estate as "a person's assets, whether they be negative or positive in value." That pretty much includes us all—though some of us might be on the uncomfortable side of the ledger! As you see, we all have estates and we all need to do some kind of planning.

Let's begin with the most basic estate planning tool: the will. Most people know about wills and fully intend to have one ... some day. However, American Bar Association surveys indicate that only 19 percent of American adults have a will or any kind of a document that directs the transfer of their property upon their death. A will allows you to design your plan to distribute your real property and other assets. It also allows you to direct the division of your estate to your family or other heirs.

Many different kinds of wills exist. My favorite one reads: "Being of sound mind ... I spent every cent I had!" However, few of us are able to gauge the length of our lifetimes. It's nearly impossible to "spend every cent" because we must keep some money for tomorrow's living expenses. No one wants to be a financial burden on family and friends. We all want to pay for our funeral expenses. Therefore, we need to do minimal planning to provide for our property after our demise and bequeath whatever remains of our estate.

Intestate Wills

In reality, people who don't have a formal will actually have chosen a will by default. That means those who don't have wills have decided to let their state government choose the manner in which their estates are disbursed. Whether or not they approve the conditions, the intestate laws of the state in which they reside at the time of their deaths have prepared wills for them. State legislatures have passed laws defining how an individual's property is to be distributed in the event of his or her death without a will. Generally, intestate laws dictate that an estate passes to the nearest relative. This may be exactly what you would want to have happen. But, too often, it isn't. That's the first reason to have your own will prepared: to ensure your wishes are carried out—not the desires of the legislature or court system.

Here's a real-life example: Catherine Marshall was suddenly thrown into unfamiliar circumstances by the death of her husband Peter Marshall, the late United States Senate Chaplain. Peter had left no will. Catherine needed to appear in probate court to inherit his estate. The law required her to post an expensive bond to be named the "Executrix and Administratrix" of Peter's affairs. Everything—all household expenses and income—became subject to the jurisdiction of the court. She couldn't pay any bills until the court approved of the expenditures—not funeral expenses, doctor or hospital bills, or even ordinary household expenses. To add insult to injury, Catherine had to appear before the probate judge to be appointed the guardian of their son, Peter John. From then on, the court required her to present detailed financial accounting of her guardianship to the court each year. This continued until her son became of age. Each year she had to pay someone to verify the accounting with a sworn statement. Plus, each year she had to pay a fee to the Office of Register of Wills for the official filing of the accounting. She was more than agitated that her husband had never "gotten around to" planning his estate. The laws thrust her into a situation that was time-consuming, costly, inconvenient, and even humiliating.

Here's another real-life example: Alfred Jackson abhorred attorneys. He wasn't about to pay one to prepare a will. He had accumulated a significant amount of savings and thought about leaving it all to his alma mater. He didn't get along well with his son and wanted to leave him nothing. Mr. Jackson died unexpectedly in an automobile accident. There was no will. Although the college knew of his intentions, they received nothing from the estate. Mr. Jackson's ne'er-do-well son inherited everything and laughed on his father's grave.

Holographic Wills

A holographic will is written entirely in a person's own handwriting. All you need is a pen and a piece of stationery or even the back of an old envelope. As long as the document is in a person's own handwriting, dated and signed by that person, most states will consider this a valid and legal instrument. A holographic will doesn't require any other formality, such as witnesses or a notary.

If you're relying on a holographic will, make sure that it's accepted by the laws of the state in which you reside. When you write a will, it's obvious that you wish people to be able to read it. If your handwriting isn't legible, you might want to type your will or have someone else prepare it for you. However, if your will isn't in your own handwriting, most states require that you have at least two witnesses and some states require three witnesses. These witnesses must be in your presence as you declare the document to be your last will and testament. They must see you sign the document. And they must be able to verify that you aren't acting under duress, you're of sound mind, and are of the age of majority (over 18 or in some cases 21).

Attorney-Prepared Wills

You may want to go a step further than the holographic will and have a professional prepare your will for you. Good reasons exist for pursuing such a course of action. For example, even though you know exactly how you want your property to be distributed, you may find it difficult to communicate your desires accurately in writing.

In another real-life example, a wealthy woman in San Diego decided to write her own will in spite of owning a large estate. Upon her death, it was discovered that in her will, she had left one-fourth of her estate to the archbishop of San Diego. A truly magnanimous gesture! But her innocent generosity created a surprising problem. An archbishop of San Diego didn't exist! The Catholic Church in Los Angeles had an archbishop but his area didn't include San Diego. Also, the Episcopal Church in San Diego had a bishop but he was not an archbishop. Those two religious organizations fought over that woman's estate. Finally, the courts decided which church would inherit her property. What a tragedy that this woman hadn't made it perfectly clear who she intended to receive her bequest. I'm sure it was clear in her mind which church she had chosen to inherit her property and benefit from her bequest. Yet a

lengthy and costly court battle ensued because of the neb-
ulous way she wrote her will. A good attorney could have
helped avoid this problem completely.

Besides designating who gets what, your will is the
place for you to name your personal representative. The
legal community used to call this person the *executor of
the estate.* Some states still do. The courts require that your
personal representative posts a bond to ensure that he will
faithfully perform the duties. A bond is simply an insurance policy to guarantee that the personal representative
will properly fulfill all the legal obligations. With a bond,
the insurance company agrees it will pay the loss in case
the personal representative misuses the representative's
authority or even absconds with the money. Obtaining a
bond is a cost to the estate. However, when writing your
will, you can allow your personal representative to act
without having to post a bond. To do this, you must state
in your will that the bond is waived.

You and your attorney can do many other things in
a written, attorney-prepared will. For example, you may
wish to leave certain assets of your estate in a testamentary
trust. This part of your will bequeaths assets to individuals who won't receive those assets immediately upon your
death. Such individuals could be minors who are ineligible
to receive an inheritance until they reach the age of majority or family members you prefer receive their share of
your estate after a certain event occurs or when they reach
a certain age. If you select a testamentary trust in which

you leave property to those who don't receive a share outright, then have an attorney assist you. These types of provisions can complicate a normal will.

Value of a Well-Written Will

This story dramatically details the value of a well-written will. After the death of a client, an attorney gathered the client's family together to read the will to them. Reading the will began by specifying several large bequests that the client had made to family members. Family members bowed their heads in modest gratitude as appropriate and uttered appreciative remarks. Then the attorney mentioned the name of a disfavored nephew. Everyone was suddenly silent. Furtive glances raced around the room like a gust of wind. The attorney cleared his throat. Without a trace of the chuckle he felt inside appearing on his face, the attorney solemnly continued to read the will: "To my nephew, whom I promised to remember, 'Hello, Charlie.'"

While this story brings a laugh, it also makes a good point. If this man had failed to write his will, nephew Charlie might have inherited everything the deceased man had owned. If Charlie had been the closest living relative, he might have walked away having uttered the appreciative remarks, eyes gleaming with anticipation of the good life ahead.

When estates are involved, remember this rule: If you don't write a will, the state will do it for you. Your will, hopefully, would meet your specific needs and wishes; the state's may not.

The Self-Proving Clause

If an attorney helps you write your will, he will likely suggest inserting details that you wouldn't have thought about such as the self-proving clause.

In the past, when a person died and left a will, the courts called back at least someone who witnessed signing the will to verify that it had been signed using proper procedures. In fact, sometimes the court called *all* the witnesses. Witnesses verified that the person who signed the will had not acted under duress or undue influence and that he had been of sound mind and of legal age. As you might imagine, often it was difficult to find all the witnesses to a will. They might have been former staff members in the law office where the client had signed the will. They might have been neighbors who had moved away. Sometimes the witnesses were deceased. But the courts required that a good faith effort be made to locate the witnesses who could verify the signing of the will.

Today, the law in many states allows you to leave language in your will (the self-proving clause) confirming that the witnesses were in your presence as you declared a document to be your last will and testament, that they saw you sign your will, they acknowledge you weren't acting under duress or undue influence of any person, and they declare that you were of proper age and of sound mind. The will includes a statement verifying these affirmations and the witnesses add their signatures, which are then notarized. This is called a self-proving will. The courts conclusively presume that self-proving wills have been properly executed. Today, the witnesses won't have to be called back into court to verify that they signed the document.

Personal Property List

An attorney might also recommend that you make a reference in your will to a separate list of tangible personal property to be distributed upon your death. This allows you to update the list from time to time without having to change your will. The list can't include real estate, stocks, bonds, cash, or business property, but it can include items of personal property such as antiques, collectibles, works of art, furniture, jewelry, and heirlooms.

This tangible personal property list can save you time and money revisiting your attorney if you change your mind about how you want to distribute a particular item. And there are countless reasons to change your mind. Let's say you have a daughter who marries John. Although you aren't thrilled with the match, you make an effort to include him in the family by leaving him something special. On your personal property list, you write: "Our grandfather clock shall be distributed to our son-in-law, John." But what if John divorces that beautiful daughter of yours? You no longer want him to receive your family's prized heirloom. You simply pull out your personal property list and remove John's name (try not to wear your

"I-knew-this-was-going-to-happen" look). Insert the name of the family member or friend you now want to receive the clock. You can do this without having to change your will. *Voila!* It's easy and free—you don't need an attorney to make the change.

✓ Action Items—Chapter 1: The LowDown on Wills

Do you have a will? Is it up to date? Take a moment to complete the following action items and keep reading for more tips and information on estate planning. After you finish reading this book, I encourage you find an attorney who specializes in estate planning.

Action 1: Create or update your will—If you don't have a will and your estate is small and uncomplicated, sit down right now and write a holographic will. Remember, holographic means this will is entirely in your own handwriting. Sign the will (no witnesses are required). If you type your will, then sign it with at least two witnesses present and have them sign it, too. If you don't have a will and you have a larger, more complicated estate (for example, if you own real estate), you may need an attorney-prepared will or trust. If you already have a will, you may need to update it soon or create a trust. Keep reading, then make an appointment with a lawyer right away—don't put it off. Don't risk putting your family through the costs and heartaches of working with the court system.

Action 2: Create or update your personal property list—Remember to include personal items such as antiques, collectibles, works of art, furniture, jewelry, and heirlooms. To distribute items such as real estate, stocks, bonds, cash, or business property, you need to work with an attorney and address those items in your will.

Go to *www.EstatePlanningDr.com/book* to download:

What to include in a holographic will (rules)

Personal Property List Form, Tips and information

A Is part of this a direct quote? If so, it should have quote marks.

Chapter Two

The Probate Factor

D o you own your own home? Do you own other real estate? Do you hold stocks, bonds, a 401(k), or other investments? Do you have dependents such as children, stepchildren, or an elderly parent? If so, perhaps your estate planning should include more than a simple will. You may need to do some additional planning. In this chapter, you'll learn about some of the misconceptions and problems concerning a simple will.

Although only 19 percent of the people who need a will actually have one, it's still the most common of all legal documents. *American Law Reports* (a legal encyclopedia) states that the will is the most likely legal document to be subject to litigation. More lawsuits are filed over wills than any other single type of legal instrument. (A)

To be effective, wills must go through a legal process called *probate*. Probate is defined as "the act or process of proving a will by a court to have competent (proper) jurisdiction." Read on to learn more about the probate process.

Stating the obvious

Probate: A procedure designed by lawyers for the benefit of lawyers.

Last night my dream turned into a nightmare.
It seemed that everything was settled out of court.

In a few exceptions, ~~with~~ *With two all* wills ~~don't~~ need to go through the probate process. One exception is when the deceased person

I had to read this sentence several times and even read the whole paragraph before I understood it. Now it is clear and

32

has held no property, either real estate or personal property, at the time of death. Another exception is when the value of an estate is less than the state's defined minimum, or statutory, amount that would require probate. In most states, this minimum amount is between $10,000 to $25,000; in Arizona, no more than $50,000; in Hawaii, $100,000. When the estate is less than the minimum amount, the assets in that estate may be transferred to a beneficiary through an affidavit, a simple procedure that doesn't require the full probate process.

Other than these two exceptions, the law says wills must be probated to distribute the assets.

The Probate Process

To more fully understand probate process requirements, let's walk through an example of how a state conducts the probate process.

We'll assume that John Doe, a widower, has died, leaving a will behind. (The process is similar whether John Doe prepared a holographic will, worked with an attorney to prepare his will, or has a de facto "will" prepared by his state legislature.) In John's will, he named his daughter, Jane, as the personal representative of the estate.

What does Jane need to do after the death of her father? First, she takes care of all the necessary funeral arrangements. Then she needs to find and review John's will. He may have a copy in his files, in a safe-deposit box, or filed at his attorney's office.

From the instructions in John's will, Jane prepares a Petition for Admission to Probate. Jane asks John's attorney to help prepare this petition. This legal document sets forth certain details, such as the date John died, the county in which he resided, and the will he left behind naming his daughter, Jane, to be the personal representative of his estate. In his will, John requested that Jane wouldn't be required to post a bond to ensure her performance. (As discussed previously, if John hadn't included a bond waiver in his will, the court would require Jane to be bonded.) This Petition for Admission to Probate lists the names, addresses, and ages of the beneficiaries of John's estate. Jane also includes an estimate of the value of all the assets John owned at the time of his death. The attorney files the petition with the clerk of the court, together with John's will (the original will, not a photocopy).

Jane then takes John's original will and the Petition for Admission to Probate to the probate judge. (In some cases, you would see a registrar who works with the probate judge's authority.) The judge reviews the will to make sure it meets all the legal requirements. If it does, the judge appoints Jane to act as the personal representative of John's estate. The judge issues his order, allowing Jane to carry out her duties as the personal representative. This authorization is usually referred to as granting Letters Testamentary.

After her appointment as the personal representative, Jane communicates with all the heirs and beneficiaries of John's estate, letting them know that the probate process has officially started. In fact, she must give this notice in writing—a phone call isn't acceptable. Jane's notice informs the heirs that she is the personal representative and provides her contact information. Her notice to the heirs tells them they have a right to know all the information about the estate. The attorney prepares an <u>Affidavit</u> of the Notice to the Heirs and Beneficiaries and files this with the probate court.

Next, Jane sends a written notice to all the creditors of the estate. Even if there are no known creditors, the law requires that the personal representative (or an attorney representing this person) publish a notice to any creditors in a newspaper of general circulation in the county in which John resided at the time of his death. (Note that an obituary notice doesn't fulfill this requirement.) It usually takes about a month from the time a probate petition is prepared and filed to the time the newspaper schedules the notice of publication. Next, the attorney prepares an <u>Affidavit</u> of the Notice to Creditors and files this with the probate court.

From the publication date, creditors have a certain period of time to file their claims against the estate. The length of time differs from state to state. In Arizona, for example, creditors are allowed four months. In other states, this allotted time ranges from three to six months. The court waives any claims that aren't presented during the specified period of time.

During this period of time, Jane can't distribute any assets from John's estate; she can't give money from John's estate to the beneficiaries or pay any creditors' bills. If Jane were to distribute any assets before all creditors' claims were filed and there wasn't enough money left in the estate to pay the valid claims, Jane would be personally liable for those claims because she's the personal representative of the estate. That's why Jane shouldn't make any distributions from John's estate until after the period of time allowed for the creditors to file their claims and after a final plan for distribution is approved, either by the court or by all the beneficiaries of the estate. As a rule, it's hazardous to pay any claims unless it's certain that sufficient funds will be available to pay expenses and all creditors. Note that probate administration expenses, including attorney's fees, usually take precedence over all other claims.

Once the period of time allowed for the creditors to file their claims passed, Jane prepares an Inventory and Appraisement of the estate—a list of the assets, and their value, that John owned at the time of his death. If Jane doesn't know their value, she may have to hire an appraiser to obtain a valuation of John's estate.

Jane must accumulate, inventory, and appraise all of John's assets. Plus, she must resolve any disputed claims or contesting of the will before she can prepare the plan to distribute the estate. When Jane creates the plan, she takes into account John's wishes (as stated in his will) to provide for his beneficiaries, the valid claims filed by John's creditors, and the probate legal and administration costs. Jane files the plan with the court and provides a copy to the beneficiaries. If the heirs agree on the distribution, Jane then distributes the property according to the plan. The probate process is now complete. In short, a "Closing Statement" is filed and the probate is terminated.

The wait in Arizona for a probate to be brought to completion averages between ten months and two years. Fortunately, some probate estates can be completed more quickly. Unfortunately, some will take much longer. I recently read about an estate that was held up in probate for 59 years! Three generations of attorneys lived off that estate and not much was left when they finally finished. That was the worst case I had heard about until I gave a presentation to a group at the Phoenix Public Library. Afterward, a gentleman walked up to me and introduced himself as a retired Philadelphia lawyer. He said he had been involved in an estate in Pennsylvania that had been open for 75 years!

Critical to Follow the Steps

It's critical to understand that you must carefully follow the steps in the probate process. Here's a real-life case study of a probate that went awry. A client of mine died and the family gathered together to divide his belongings. Family members discovered one of the major items in his estate: a box full of gold coins of great value. The family distributed the coins among my client's daughters, who quickly sold them and spent the money.

However, as required, the representative of the estate had listed the gold coins as an asset of the estate on the probate records. To make matters worse, with the gold coins gone, the estate didn't have enough money left to pay the valid claims. Julie, the daughter who had been named the personal representative, became personally liable to pay those claims herself. Luckily, Julie was able to convince her sisters to repay the estate, which left sufficient monies to pay the claims. But while Julie alone was liable for the creditors' claims, it was an uncomfortable, stressful situation for her.

Happily, these are extreme examples. Even Howard Hughes's estate took only 11 years to settle, a short period of time when you consider that 32 wills were presented to the Texas and Nevada courts after his death. Not one was found to be valid. The Nevada attorney fees alone amounted to $8,500,000.

In addition to the fact that probate can be a lengthy process, probate records are not private and confidential. Anyone can enter the courthouse and ask to see the probate file for any deceased person. You may review the probate file whether you're a nosey neighbor, a disgruntled heir, or a newspaper reporter. For example, after the death of Natalie Wood, *The Wall Street Journal* sent a reporter to review her probate file. It published an article that Natalie's estate was worth $6,000,000 and included, among other things, 29 fur coats. This juicy tidbit was available for anyone to discover because her estate was settled through probate. When you settle an estate through probate, don't expect privacy.

The High Costs of Probate

Legal costs pose another major problem in the probate process. Costs include filing fees with the court and publication costs as well as potential appraisal fees, bond fees, administrative costs, and other miscellaneous expenses. I hate to even bring up the most obvious cost: attorneys' fees. (I can't pass this opportunity for a little attorney humor: An attorney was once described as "a learned gentleman who rescues your estate from your enemies—and keeps it for himself!")

Nationwide, the average probate costs between 5 and 10 percent of the estate, most of which is attorneys' fees. In an interview with a Scottsdale newspaper, an Arizona probate attorney estimated that an average probate attorney's fee in Arizona ranged between $5,000 and $10,000. *Money* magazine published an article concerning the nation's probate problems. Its investigative reporters calculated that an average estate worth $200,000 would cost 5 percent, or $10,000, to settle (from "Revocable Living Trusts," *Money*, December 1985).

How Much is the Attorney's Fee?

While investigating the cost of estate planning, I conducted a survey among estate planning attorneys nationwide. My questionnaire asked their average legal fee to handle an estate and how they arrived at this fee. I included questions regarding the time delays in the settlement of the estate as well as the costs involved. Below are some of the responses I received.

- Fifty-eight percent of the responding attorneys said they based their fees on a percentage of the estate.
- An attorney from Missouri indicated that the time delays varied according to the problems encountered in the estate. His added note described his experience with common probate problems: "Number-one problem: litigation. Number two: the tax liabilities of the estate. Third: court backlog (which is becoming more and more prevalent). Fourth: lawyer backlog!" This lawyer added that his minimum fee to settle an estate is $2,500 and increases with the size of the estate.

- A Maryland attorney also had a base fee of $2,500, but the fee could escalate to over $50,000, depending on the size of the estate. On average, he charged 15 percent of the value of the estate. He estimated that it takes, on average, 12 to 36 months to settle an estate.
- A response from Texas indicated a base fee was only $1,500, but depending on the assets, the fee increases to $25,000 or more.
- A Georgia lawyer listed $7,500 as a minimum fee.

The responses to this survey clearly showed an unsympathetic attitude shared by the lawyers relating to the high cost, the average duration, and even the drawn-out length of time involved in the whole probate process. Remember, a revocable living trust will help you avoid all these problems.

Action Items—Chapter 2: The Probate Factor

Take a moment to complete the following action items and keep reading for more information on estate planning.

Action 1: Call your lawyer—If you currently have a will, ask your attorney how long the probate process typically takes in your county. Also, ask how the fee is determined to settle an estate and what the fee would be for your estate.

Action 2: Review your will—If you currently have a will, take it out of the file and read it.

Do you need to change your beneficiaries?

Do you need to update the real estate and investment assets described?

Do you need to change your personal representative?

Familiarize yourself with the terms of your current will; this is the heart of your current estate plan. Keep these points in mind as you read the following chapters on trusts. *Excellent way to say "keep reading"*

Go to *www.EstatePlanningDr.com/book* to download:

Will Analysis Form

Chapter Three

Trusts versus Wills

A re you familiar with a situation in which someone died and no probate process followed? In the settlement of that estate, the heirs wouldn't have encountered the problems mentioned in the previous chapter because several ways exist to avoid most of those problems.

One way is called a *trust*. Using a living trust is becoming the most popular way to avoid going through probate. Now, don't get distracted by the word *trust*. Many people are apprehensive of this word because it seems to be inexorably related to the word *estate*. Often, *estate* conjures up a picture of a large plantation complete with rolling hills, oil wells in the backyard, and a Rolls Royce parked in front of the four-car garage.

Yes, that's one definition of *estate*. If you have this type of an estate, you'll need serious estate planning and that's when it's especially important to have a trust. You may be thinking, "Of course, if a trust is involved, a bank must be acting as the trustee." Whoa! Slow down! While the common perception about using a trust is that it's just for the wealthy, this simply isn't true. Those of us with smaller "estates" can also greatly benefit from using a trust.

Who Manages the Trust?

Many people are uneasy about putting their estates into a trust because they believe only a bank can be the manager or trustee of their trust. Also not true! Yet this misconception is amazingly prevalent. Recently, I was giving a presentation about wills and trusts to members of an Optimist Club. A friend of mine, an attorney, attended the meeting. At one point in the presentation, he raised his hand and asked, "Steve, why don't you tell these people why many of us attorneys recommend that our clients don't set up trusts?"

I wasn't sure what he meant so I replied, "Well, Keith, why don't you tell them?"

He responded, "Most of my clients are adamant about wanting to retain control over their property. They don't want to give it up and put it in the hands of a bank, a trust company, or even their friendly neighborhood attorney."

I was shocked to discover that my friend—an attorney—didn't fully understand how trusts work. I had the distinct pleasure of informing the group, along with my friend, that *you* can be the trustee of your own trust. You don't need a bank or trust company to act as trustee unless that's what you want. Judging from my friend's comment, many people are probably in the dark about trusts.

Let's turn up the light and discuss trusts.

Different Names for a Trust

Trusts have different names. A "living" trust is established while you're living—the trust must do what you would want it to do upon your death, as if you were still living.

A living trust is sometimes referred to as an *inter vivos trust*. *Inter vivos* is Latin for *between the living*. (Some people believe it sounds more prestigious if you use the Latin terminology.) Promoters might call this type of trust a *loving trust* because it promotes love and unity among the family. It's often referred to as a *revocable trust* or a *revocable living trust* because you may alter, amend, or even revoke the trust during your lifetime.

This is the opposite of an *irrevocable trust*, which you can't alter, amend, or revoke after it has been established. Some people refer to the living trust as a *grantor trust* because the person who establishes the trust is the grantor who retains control during his lifetime. They're talking about the same kind of trust with the same characteristics, so don't be concerned about the different terminology.

Basic Requirements

Let's review the basic requirements and parameters of a trust:

1. A trust must be in writing—The document must outline, elucidate, describe, and incorporate all of its terms.
2. A trust must have a grantor—Also called the *settlor* or *trustor,* this is the person setting up the trust.
3. The trust must have a trustee—This is the manager who controls, operates, and manages all the property held in the trust.
4. The trust must have a beneficiary—This person or persons inherit the estate.

My Family's Trust

I have set up a revocable living trust for my family so I'll use that as an example to describe how a trust operates. Of course, my trust is in writing. I am the settlor because I established or settled the trust. I didn't want a bank or trust company acting as trustee for my trust. I wish to remain in full control of my assets, so I am the trustee. I manage my own trust. I can still buy, sell, reinvest, or give away any trust assets without the approval of any bank. I've transferred all my property into the trust.

How a Living Trust works.

I'm married and my wife Linda joined me in setting up our trust. She also joined in the transfer of property into the trust. Therefore, she is a co-settlor and a co-trustee.

[handwritten annotation: Without the commas, means you have more than one wife. ☺]

My wife has as much to say about the use of that trust property as I do. In the event that something happens to me, she can continue to manage the trust without any further changes. (You don't need to have a co-trustee if you are single or simply don't wish to have a co-trustee.)

If we both die in a common disaster, we've named a third person to carry on with the revocable living trust, called the *successor trustee*. Many people will name a bank or a trust company as successor trustee because these institutions have experience and expertise in trust management. Again, you can name anyone you desire as successor trustee; you don't have to name a bank or trust company to that position.

With my brother's consent, my wife and I originally named him as our successor trustee. Besides the family ties, we chose Jim because he shares our beliefs regarding raising children and making investment decisions. (In return, I was appointed to be the successor trustee of his revocable living trust.) However, now that our children are grown, my wife and I reconsidered our selection of successor trustee. We have complete confidence in our oldest daughter Kari, a paralegal, and have amended our trust to name her the successor trustee.

Finally, our trust agreement names the beneficiaries of the trust: our children. They will receive our property in the event of both our deaths. However, when all our children were under age 18, they couldn't receive an outright inheritance of that property. Any inheritance had to be held in trust for them. Even when our children reached age 18, my wife and I still didn't want them to receive an outright inheritance. In our trust, we've designated that our children will receive the property in a three-tiered distribution. They will receive a portion at the time of our deaths (but only if they are over age 25); another share five years later; and a final distribution ten years after our deaths. Our objective is to ensure they'll wisely handle their inheritance as they mature.

Choose Wise Money Managers

Through the experiences of some of my clients, I've learned that young people often aren't wise money managers. Recently, a couple came into my office to do some estate planning and set up a trust. While conversing, they shared a sad story. Their son, Tom, died about three years ago. His property had gone through a probate, which took about two years. At the time of the settlement, Tom's oldest son was 19. He received an outright distribution of $30,000 from the settlement of Tom's father's estate. My clients, Tom's grandparents, reported that only one year after the distribution, Tom's son didn't have a penny left of that inheritance. He had spent it all and had nothing to show for it. This often happens when someone receives an inheritance but isn't mature enough for the responsibility. That's precisely why our children will receive their inheritance in a three-tiered distribution.

Although our children won't receive an outright distribution until they reach the specified ages, they'll still have the immediate benefit of the trust. My daughter, who is 33 years old, has the right to use all the income as successor trustee. She has access to as much of the principal in the trust as necessary for the daily maintenance, care, and education of our children. She can pay for their medical expenses, education costs, and general costs of wellbeing without needing to go to court to receive approval to release any funds.

Even though we've declared in our trust that our children won't receive an outright inheritance, our property won't be tied up in the courts. It's available for immediate use by the successor trustee to benefit our children—without probate. In addition, the settlement of our estate remains private.

Schedule of Trust Assets

Attached to the trust is a schedule of trust assets, an itemized list of all the property that has been transferred to the trust. Our family's schedule of trust assets describes and identifies our home, bank accounts, investments, and other personal property items. Obviously, we need to adjust this list from time to time when we sell, reinvest, change, or purchase assets.

It's easy to keep the schedule up to date. For example, you may have your investments in a certificate of deposit (CD). When it matures, merely write on your schedule of trust assets that you cashed out the CD and note the date. Then, if you purchase another investment, simply add a description of the new asset to your schedule of trust assets to keep your list current.

When my wife and I transferred our property into our trust, we took that property out of our own names and put it into the name of the trust, showing both of us as co-trustees. We still have full control, use, and management of that property, but it's no longer in our names. In the event of our deaths, no assets are in our personal names—no property or investments are under our ownership to go through the probate process. Remember, if a person has no real or personal property in his name at the time of death, *there is no probate*. Probate gets eliminated completely. Because there is no probate, the property isn't tied up in the court system and unavailable for use. By setting up a trust, we've eliminated the time—an average of ten months to two years—that our heirs must wait for our property to be distributed.

[handwritten margin notes: and initial the entry. (See pg 52) Do you need to do so when you "add" a new item?]

Buying and Selling Our Home—a Trust Asset

Some time after my wife and I set up our revocable living trust, we wanted to sell our home, the title of which was held by our trust. No problem. Of course, the title company needed to know that we had the right to sell our house so we showed them a copy of the trust. (My daughter, the successor trustee, also knows the details of the trust. However, it remains a private document.) We had listed our home on our trust's schedule of trust assets, so next to the description of the home on the schedule, we marked it as sold, entered the date of the sale, and initialed the entry. We deposited the money received from the sale of the house into a bank account that was already in the trust's name and on the schedule of trust assets. Eventually, we bought a new home with that money and added a description of the new home onto the schedule of trust assets. At the close of escrow, we put the deed to our new home in the name of our trust.

Another great benefit of a trust is the privacy factor. When my wife and I die, no one will need to file our trust with the court. Or record it. Or make it a matter of public record. It's a private document. Only those who have a need to know will be given information about our trust.

The privacy issue is certainly beneficial. However, the most important consideration in choosing between using a trust or will is generally bottom-line costs. An attorney can prepare an average will for $400 to $500 and set up an *were these prices correct at the time of publica-tion? 2007 (also refers to the it's on the rest of this page, involved*

average trust for about $2,000 to $2,500. (Of course, those costs depend on the attorney you hire and the complexities of your particular estate.) It doesn't require a CPA to immediately figure that it costs five times more to set up the average trust versus the average will. The key words here are "set up." The prices I just quoted are for exactly that—"setting up" your will or trust. Those up-front costs don't include the cost of administering your wishes after your death.

When you die, what does it cost to carry out your carefully laid plans? Many people believe it's simply the cost to *that the only fee* create the document that plans their estate: their will or trust. If your attorney draws up a will for you, it may cost $400. However, upon your death, your estate goes through the probate process. Then the fees for settling your estate could easily reach $10,000 (the average cost of probate). Now the total cost of settling your estate isn't $400—it's a whopping $10,400. This explains why a will is one of the most expensive legal documents in this country.

Remember that the average trust costs $2,000 to $2,500 to set up, but there's no probate. A trust eliminates the total cost of probate and that potential $10,000 probate fee. Plus, your successor trustee has the immediate right to distribute your property according to the plan described in your trust. He doesn't have to go to a court or even hire an attorney to settle the estate.

Your successor trustee might feel unsure about how to distribute your property according to your trust and want to have some counsel and advice. Often, the successor trustee will go to an attorney to review the trust document and learn how to proceed. Let's assume this happens. The attorney visits with the successor trustee and may prepare some transfer documents. The attorney charges a few hundred dollars for this service. (The average fee to review and help settle an estate with a trust is about $500.) Now the total cost of your estate plan is $2,500. Compare this to using a will for your estate plan, which would cost $10,400. It doesn't take a CPA to figure out that a will can actually costs four times more than a trust!

Remember, of all legal documents, a will is the most likely to be contested. It's also one of the most expensive legal documents because of the total costs to settle an estate.

The Perils of Probate

Recently, the following letter appeared in our local newspaper:

"Dear Editor,

In his recent column offering legal comment as a supposed public service, [a Phoenix lawyer] candidly acknowledges that much of the public's animosity toward lawyers derives from the skinning that a deceased person's heirs receive in the probate process. Amen to that sentiment. I have recently endured the process of settling a simple, solvent estate of relatively small size and with only one heir ..."

My initial response to this letter was one of shock: Is there really public animosity toward lawyers? (All right, I admit I already knew the answer to that question.) But the overwhelming truth of the letter is frightening. The writer declares that this is a small, simple estate, meaning the process shouldn't be complicated. And the writer clarifies that it's a solvent estate, meaning there aren't any creditors to worry about. An estate "with only one heir" indicates no one will bicker over the property.

The writer continues his comments about an attorney's column in the paper:

"... I was mulched of nearly $10,000 in attorney's fees. I invite those who would fancy a protracted adventure into the Byzantine complexities of the law to have a go at probate. They would see the legal process at its larcenist worst. What [the attorney] could have told his legally naive readers is that one can have a so-called living trust drawn and thereby avoid virtually all the preposterous, make work, flapdoodle of a probated will. The trust is easy, quick, and cheap. Moreover, it is private and avoids the needless spreading of a dead loved one's personal and business affairs throughout the courthouse records."

The letter was signed: Robert W. Blair, MD.

To Mr. Blair, I emphatically reply, "Hear! Hear!" Perhaps a similar experience inspired Charles Hughes Evans to declare, "The United States is the greatest law factory the world has ever known."

The Story of Mrs. Will and Mrs. Trust

Mr. Blair's letter reminded me of an experience I had many years ago. I had opened my office as a sole practitioner and I wasn't yet an experienced estate planning attorney. In one month, two elderly widows each requested my legal assistance. As far as I know, the ladies had never met and they didn't meet at my office. Both ladies had similar problems. In fact, the similarities of their respective situations made these events memorable.

I'll refer to the first lady as Mrs. Will. She said, "Mr. Allen, I've been to see a doctor and he tells me that I'm suffering from terminal cancer. I have only four or five months left to live. I want to have a new will drawn so I can leave my property to my family and have everything organized upon my death."

Even for a lawyer, those are hard words to hear. As we visited, I learned that she had an average-size estate. She wasn't wealthy, but she owned her own home; had some stocks and bonds, bank accounts, and CDs; and owned various other property. She owned a parcel of real estate in Colorado and she owned interesting personal items—including an antique-doll collection, with which her granddaughter Sarah had fallen in love. Mrs. Will specifically wanted to leave the doll collection to Sarah. I prepared a will for her, which we later reviewed together. When she signed it, she went her way, thinking her estate had been adequately put in order.

The second widow who called me that month asked me to come to her home. She required an oxygen machine and it was difficult for her to get around. I'll refer to her as Mrs. Trust. It was distressing to hear her utter almost the exact same news that Mrs. Will had divulged only a few days earlier, saying, "Mr. Allen, my doctor tells me that I'm suffering from terminal cancer. I have only about four months left to live. I want to put my estate in order and leave it to my family."

Mrs. Trust's estate was about the same size as Mrs. Will's estate. Mrs. Trust owned her home, had some bank accounts and other investments, and had a few treasured personal items. She wasn't wealthy, but she wanted what she possessed to be left to her family. However, Mrs. Trust had one other request. She said, "We've only recently completed the probate of my deceased husband's estate. He died three years ago. His probate was closed just last year. I don't want my children to go through that process upon my death. What do you recommend?"

I suggested she set up a simple revocable living trust. And that's exactly what we did. It was similar to the trust my wife and I set up years later. Mrs. Trust transferred her property into her trust: her home, bank accounts, and other investments. We listed everything on the Schedule of Trust Assets. She named herself as the trustee, she named one of her sons to act as successor trustee in the event of her death, and she named all her children as equal beneficiaries. She signed the trust and transfer documents, satisfied that her affairs were now in order.

Settling Mrs. Will's Estate

As the doctor predicted, Mrs. Will died about four months later. Her son came to see me and said, "Mr. Allen, we know you prepared a will for Mother. She died last week; we'd like you to handle the probate of her estate." I began the probate process. Remember what this involves: I had to prepare a Petition for Admission to Probate, listing the information concerning Mrs. Will's estate. This included names and address of all beneficiaries of the will, Mr. Will's name and address as personal representative, and an estimate of the value of the estate. Together with the will, I took this petition downtown and filed it with the court. I went to see the probate judge, who reviewed the petition and the will. He found everything to be in order and named Mr. Will to act as the personal representative. I prepared the Notice to Creditors and the Notice to Beneficiaries. Mr. Will began listing the property in his mother's estate for the Inventory and Appraisement required by the court.

About three weeks later, Mr. Will ran into my office. Agitated, he demanded, "Mr. Allen, what have you done to me?"

Not sure myself, I responded, "I don't know, what have I done?"

He explained that several years earlier, he had been divorced. At that time, he was living in another state. The court in that state had ordered him to pay child support and alimony. He didn't want to pay child support and alimony so he had moved to Arizona and had been in hiding from his ex-wife ever since. In an interesting quirk of fate, the daughter for whom this man had refused to pay child support was Sarah, the granddaughter who was to receive Mrs. Will's antique doll collection. Sarah was one of the named beneficiaries.

I had done my job and acquired Sarah's address. Per my responsibility, I had sent her notice of her grandmother's death. Sarah was living with her mother, the Ex-Mrs. Will, who now knew where her ex-husband was residing. She immediately filed a lawsuit against Mr. Will to collect back payments for the child support and alimony he owed. For this, Mr. Will was angry with me.

I explained, "Mr. Will, just because you've violated the court order doesn't mean that I can disobey the law. I have to give notice of your mother's death to creditors and to the beneficiaries. Your daughter was one of them. I suggest you pay the back child support and alimony." He eventually complied, but he was extremely unhappy with the whole process.

In the process of probating the estate, I had published the Notice to Creditors. I received several creditors' claims against Mrs. Will's estate. I had found evidence of the existence of several of those claims in her records so I knew she had contracted for those debts, services, or products. But other creditors submitted claims for which I had found no record; those claims were disallowed. Some of the creditors whose claims were disallowed filed an action within the probate court to have their claims allowed. This required additional hearings at the courthouse. We had to hear witnesses and produce evidence, which required additional time. Eventually, the judge allowed some of those claims and disallowed others. All this cost the estate additional money and time delays.

In addition, Mrs. Will owned property: her summer home in Colorado. When you own real property in another state, a probate is required in that state as well. Yes, that's right—a second probate. So we had to hire a Colorado attorney and have him begin an ancillary probate in the state of Colorado. This step immediately doubled the attorneys' fees to settle the estate. The attorney eventually sold the Colorado property, we transferred the money received for the sale into the Arizona probate, and closed the ancillary probate. At long last, I thought we were ready to close out the Arizona probate and distribute the remaining assets.

I prepared a plan for distribution based on the will that Mrs. Will had dictated. I filed this plan with the court and sent it to the heirs. However, some of the heirs didn't agree with this plan, and wouldn't approve it. For that reason, Mrs. Will's estate wasn't settled until the court entered its own decision on the matter of distribution. Several years had passed since Mrs. Will's death. Because the family never agreed on the plan for distribution, this developed hard feelings among the siblings. Some of them still don't speak to each other.

I think you get the picture … and it's not a pretty one. It seems that something happened at every step in the probate of Mrs. Will's estate to cause additional delay, cost to the estate, and disagreement: the disputed creditor claims, the unpaid alimony and child support, the Colorado property requiring a Colorado ancillary probate, and the disagreement about the final distribution of property.

Settling Mrs. Trust's Estate

Thankfully, the ending to Mrs. Trust's story is much simpler and happier for her family. When she died (about the same time as Mrs. Will did) her son *(Mr. Trust)* came to see me. He asked, "Mr. Allen, we know you prepared this trust for Mother; we'd like to distribute the property. I'm named the successor trustee. What do I need to do?" I reviewed the trust document with him and explained his duties as the successor trustee. He asked me to help prepare some of the legal documents to transfer some of the property. Within two weeks, Mrs. Trust's estate was fully settled and completely distributed. The fees I charged for my involvement were extremely small. Mr. Trust felt good about his experience and the settlement of his mother's estate.

Trust the Trust!

I learned a lot from settling those two estates. Now, whenever someone comes into my law office and declares, "Mr. Allen, I'd like to have a will drawn," I explain some of the problems often linked with wills. I detail the probate process: It may take one to two years, or more, to settle the will. It may cost between 5 and 10 percent of the value of the estate, or more. Probate records are open to the public and the settlement won't remain private.

Many people are unaware of all the problems that probate causes. They're also unaware that they can avoid probate by using a revocable living trust. Most of my clients have learned to trust the trust! Yet some people still want to have their estate planned with the use of a will. That's fine with me. At least I know they're making an educated decision and I'm happy to prepare a will for them.

I wish I had explained trusts to Mrs. Will. If I had, she may have chosen a revocable living trust instead of a will. This would have eliminated the probate in both Colorado and Arizona by transferring both pieces of real property to one trust. (A trust can hold property in more than one state.) We would have been able to distribute the property in her estate within a short period of time after her death. Perhaps Mrs. Will's heirs would still be speaking to each other.

///

Action Items—Chapter 3: Trusts vs Wills

Take a moment to complete the following action items.

Action 1: How would your heirs be affected by the probate process?—Do a quick estimate of the current value of your estate including the equity in your home, your investments, and other property. Then ask yourself this question: "If both my spouse and I tragically die tomorrow, how will the probate process affect our estate and, more important, impact our heirs?" Using this chapter as a guide, write down the implications to your heirs if they had to weather a lengthy, expensive probate process.

Action 2: How would your heirs be affected by the trust process?—Again, using this chapter as a guide, reflect on how the fast, relatively inexpensive revocable living trust would affect your estate and your heirs.

Thinking about one's own mortality may make this a challenging exercise. However, by putting yourself in Mrs. Will and Mrs. Trust's places, the ramifications of wills and trusts hit home.

Go to *www.EstatePlanningDr.com/book* to download:

List of Current Assets

///

Chapter Four

"Trust Me ..."

B y now, you see how a revocable living trust is an excellent tool to avoid the hassle and excess costs of probate. But circumventing the probate issue isn't the only advantage of establishing a revocable living trust. This kind of trust:

- Helps you avoid paying excess taxes.
- Addresses the issue of your becoming mentally or physically incapacitated (the most neglected problem in estate planning).
- Helps you select the best type of power of attorney.
- Helps you face the reality of the importance of a living will.
- Addresses the issue that, legally, a minor child is considered an incapacitated person.
- Allows professionals who hold stock in their own corporation to protect the corporation from serious loss of value in the event of that person's death.

- Solves the problems inherent in joint tenancy, right of survivorship, and community property.

Let's investigate these issues in depth.

Paying Excess Federal Estate Taxes

One significant cost of settling an estate is often over-looked: the federal estate tax. Unfortunately, most of us don't have to deal with that problem. I say *unfortunately* because few of us have an estate worth over $2 million—the current amount exempt from federal estate tax. Note the applicable exclusion amount for United States federal estate taxes, presented in Figure 4.1

For the year:	The Applicable Exclusion Amount for U.S. Federal Estate Taxes
2000 and 2001	$675,000
2002 and 2003	$1 million
2004 and 2005	$1.5 million
2006 to 2008	$2 million
2009	$3.5 million
2010	N/A (taxes repealed!)
2011	$1 million

Figure 4.1—The applicable exclusion rate for United States federal estate taxes. If you die in the year 2007, for example, your estate is exempt from federal estate taxes if it's valued at less than $2 million. Notice that the applicable exclusion amount increases through the year 2009, meaning that estates with higher values become exempt from paying federal estate taxes.

If you're married and have a large estate, you can use a trust to allow both spouses to retain that $2 million exemption. Through your trust, you may protect up to $4 million from any federal estate tax and, furthermore, reduce the tax that is assessed on anything over that amount.

Notice in the applicable exclusion amount chart that the exclusion amount increases to $3.5 million in the year 2009. The next year, the federal estate tax is repealed altogether. The IRS won't impose an estate tax on those who die in the year 2010. At this time, this repeal isn't permanent. Unless Congress votes to extend this repeal, the IRS will assess an estate tax once again in the year 2011. To make matters worse, the exclusion amount will revert to what it was in 2003: only $1 million! This can seriously affect many people's estates; if you die and have $1 million in assets, your heirs can be heavily taxed by the federal estate tax.

To help reduce estate taxes, married couples have an *unlimited marital deduction*. Many people are confused by this phrase. It means that upon the death of either spouse, there is an unlimited marital deduction—no estate tax is imposed at that time. Because of this marital deduction, the surviving spouse won't have to pay any taxes on the value of the assets left behind. This is true no matter the size of the estate, whether it's valued at $10,000 or $10 million. The IRS doesn't assess tax at the death of the first spouse.

Revocable Living Trust with A/B provision.

However, upon the death of the second spouse, all the assets get included in that person's taxable estate. The second spouse to die enjoys only one federal estate tax exemption of $2 million. In short, a married couple experiences only one federal estate tax exemption of $2 million—not an exemption of $2 million for each spouse.

Here's where the trusty trust can make a huge difference in the amount of inheritance you're able to leave to your beneficiaries. Let's say you and your spouse have asked your attorney to set up a revocable living trust with a provision for an A/B trust (this type of trust is sometimes referred to as a *marital deduction trust*). By using an A/B trust, a married couple retains the applicable exclusion amount for each spouse. With an A/B trust, upon the death of either spouse, the trust assets may be split into two shares: Share A (the survivor's share) and Share B (the decedent's share). Each share retains the $2 million exemption.

This is how an A/B trust works: The surviving spouse has full and complete use of all the income and principal of Share A (the survivor's share) of the trust. The surviving spouse also has the right to all the income of Share B (the decedent's share) of the trust. In addition, the surviving spouse may use as much of the principal of Share B as necessary to maintain such spouse's current standard of living or to provide for any illness or accident. The A/B trust has one simple stipulation: The surviving spouse can use the principal from Share B only after the principal from Share A has been exhausted. Because the decedent's share has been locked in and can't be used except for emergency or necessity, both shares are allowed to retain that $2 million federal tax exemption. By using a simple revocable living trust with A/B split, the total federal tax exemption can be doubled to $4 million! And beautifully, the surviving spouse may still retain control and make all investments and other decisions affecting the trust.

If you currently have a living trust that doesn't include this provision, you may add an A/B trust with an amendment or trust restatement. To determine if your trust has an A/B trust election, search the table of contents of your living trust for "separate trusts" or a similar description.

Becoming Mentally or Physically Incapacitated

A revocable living trust can be your safety net should you become incapacitated. Perhaps the best way to present the benefits of a trust in this area is to share a personal experience.

Several years ago, a woman I'll call Mrs. Banks made an appointment with me. She requested that I prepare a revocable living trust for her $250,000 estate. She wanted to leave it to her family without going through the hassles of probate. I prepared the trust and notified her that it was ready for her signature. Before she could come in to sign it, she was involved in a car accident. This placed her in the hospital for several months—physically incapacitated and mentally unable to handle her own affairs.

Mrs. Banks's neighbor, Mr. Nosey, was a close friend. Before the accident, he'd been helping her with investments and tax planning. He was legitimately concerned that she wasn't able to pay her bills over this extended period of time. Mr. Nosey and his attorney friend decided they should ask the court to appoint a conservator to pay Mrs. Banks's bills and take care of her other needs. Mr. Nosey and his attorney friend filed a request with the court to name a conservator. The process is similar to a probate process and is, therefore, often referred to as a *living probate*. An attorney must file a Petition for Appointment of Conservator, give notices to creditors, compile an inventory and accounting, and so on.

Since Mr. Nosey had previously been helping Mrs. Banks with her estate (paying the taxes, etc.), he was well versed on the condition of her property and could compile a fairly complete picture of her assets. And when Mr. Nosey and his attorney applied to the court for help, the court responded. The judge appointed a social worker to be the guardian for Mrs. Banks, to visit her at the hospital, and to make sure her physical needs were being met. The court also ordered that a bank be appointed as the trustee of Mrs. Banks's property. The judge required that the bank would have its attorneys draw up a trust agreement for Mrs. Banks. Then the court, with the help of the bank's attorneys, would transfer all of Mrs. Banks's property over to this court-approved trust. The bank would then begin to pay her bills.

Happily, after some time, Mrs. Banks began to recover and was eventually able to return home. But what was her state of affairs? Not as she had left them. Her Cadillac had been sold. Her furs were placed in storage somewhere. She wasn't able to account for all her jewelry and other items. She was allowed a meager weekly living allowance of $175. Poor Mrs. Banks. This was an unsatisfactory situation.

In frustration, she came to me for advice to regain control over her own property. The first time I'd heard of her deplorable situation was at this meeting. Mrs. Banks brought with her the court documents to show what had happened. I explained that she needed to have the court-approved trust "set aside" or overturned. To do this, she needed to see the doctor who declared her incapacitated and have him verify that she had recovered.

Mrs. Banks did so. She made an appointment with the doctor, who examined her and asked her to respond to questions on a series of tests. Because these tests were critically important to her personal freedom, the poor woman was under severe pressure and became flustered. She had a difficult time with one test: an exercise in counting backward. The doctor asked her questions about specific dates, events, persons, and places in her life to which he knew the answers. Tragically, Mrs. Banks couldn't recall everything and was unable to offer complete answers. The doctor was reluctant to sign a letter stating she had fully recovered.

At the court hearing regarding her conservatorship, Mrs. Banks felt much more like herself. When the judge interviewed her on the witness stand, she responded normally. But because the doctor hadn't signed the letter stating she had fully recovered, the judge was reluctant to set aside that court-approved trust and return her own property to Mrs. Banks. The judge did increase her living allowance, but the court-appointed bank continued to serve as trustee of her trust and control her assets.

About 18 months later, I learned of Mrs. Banks's death. I believe that a broken spirit and a broken heart—brought about by loss of control over her own property—seriously contributed to her demise. It was doubly sad to realize that if she had been able to sign the revocable living trust I had prepared for her, Mrs. Banks's daughter could have taken over the management of her mother's property. When Mrs. Banks had recovered sufficiently, the daughter could have turned the property back to her mother's charge. The family could have handled the whole disturbing affair easily, without the costly and extensive courtroom procedure. And who knows? Mrs. Banks might still be alive today. This dramatic story reveals how powerful and valuable a trust can be—not just when someone dies but also if someone becomes incapacitated.

A revocable living trust completely eliminates the need for a conservatorship. In your own trust, you may specify that you'll act as trustee until your death, disability, or legal incapacity. And in the event of your incapacity, name someone to act as the successor trustee. Your successor trustee will be able to take over the management of your trust without being appointed by the court. I believe mental or physical incapacity is one of the most neglected problems in estate planning. A revocable living trust will protect you from this contingency.

At the Mercy of the Court

A celebrated figure who didn't get around to planning his estate was Groucho Marx. In his later years, Groucho had become incapacitated and completely dependent on others. At the time, a young woman, Erin Fleming, lived with Groucho and cared for his needs. She needed to have authority granted to her by the court to enable her to provide for certain basic needs and manage the household. So she applied for a conservatorship. When Erin Fleming sought the appointment, she was opposed by some of Marx's shirttail relatives. As Groucho sat despondently in the courtroom, the judge appointed a bank as the trustee of his estate and required that a written trust be created. The trust was approved, which eventually left the estate to these shirttail relatives upon Groucho's death. No one knows if Groucho wanted to leave his estate to Erin Fleming or his shirttail relatives. But if Groucho had done basic planning, he would have made that decision himself instead of being at the mercy of a court.

Power of Attorney

One of the benefits of a trust is that it gives authority to the successor trustee to act for the settlor if the settlor/ trustee becomes incapacitated. (Note that the settlor and trustee are usually the same person.) The trust agreement grants the successor trustee the power to manage the trust and its assets for the benefit of the incapacitated trustee if a disability occurs. However, the successor trustee must prove such an incapacity with a letter from the settlor's medical doctor. To successfully request this letter from the doctor, the trust agreement must grant this authority to the successor trustee. This required language, often referred to as the *HIPAA language*, is mandated by the Federal Health Insurance Portability and Accountability Act (HIPAA). When this language is part of trust agreement, the medical doctor is specifically authorized to share the respective medical records with the successor trustee. If this language isn't in the trust agreement, the successor trustee must go to court, ask a judge for permission to act on behalf of the trust, and show a good reason for the court to grant this authority. (Doctors who release medical records without the proper authority are subject to penalties and fines.)

In many instances, it's easier to use a power of attorney to allow the successor trustee to manage the trust assets. This is especially true if the trustee is expected to be incapacitated for a short duration. For example, the trustee may plan to undergo a medical operation or simply be out of town for an extended period of time and may need someone to manage certain actions regarding a trust asset. Many unforeseen reasons exist to grant a power of attorney to the person named as successor trustee.

*This was a lot easier before they were
so concerned about protecting the identity
of the patient.*

A power of attorney is an instrument authorizing someone else to act as your agent or attorney-in-fact. With a power of attorney, you name someone to act in your place, name, and stead as your agent. For example, you may need someone to pay your bills if you're unable to do so.

A power of attorney may be general (broad or all inclusive) or special (limited to certain uses). It may become effective immediately or become valid upon your disability (this is called a *springing power of attorney*). After the HIPAA law was passed, springing power of attorney became essentially useless because it creates such a dilemma: Your agent can't act on your behalf unless you're proven to be incapacitated. You can't be proven to be incapacitated without your medical records. Your agent doesn't have access to your medical records without the express authority mandated by the HIPAA law—or a court order. So the question becomes, "How can this springing power of attorney spring into effect?" It's a Catch-22.

A power of attorney is void upon your death and also upon your disability—unless you direct that it be effective even in the event of your disability (this is called a *durable power of attorney*). You may combine the characteristics you need into one power of attorney. I've found the most suitable power of attorney is this: general durable power of attorney.

It's a good idea to update your power of attorney about every two to three years. Most banks look at an older power of attorney as being stale and won't honor it. Some banks even require that a power of attorney be declared on a pre-printed form and not be older than two years. Check with your bank regarding its requirements. Note, though, that a bank's requirements may be the bank's policy, not legal requirements. However, it's not easy to argue with a bank about the appropriateness of its policies or the legality of your legal documents. It's easier just to go along with your bank's policy.

The state of Arizona has recognized the problem of requiring regular updates to your power of attorney. The Arizona legislature has approved a law stating a power of attorney is valid "… regardless of how much time has elapsed, unless the instrument states a definite termination time."

Living Will

Preparing your living trust reminds you that you won't be here forever. You may become incapacitated before you die. If you know you don't want to be kept on life support just to prolong the dying process, you must prepare a living will.

A living will is a document that expresses your desire to not be kept on artificial, life-prolonging, medical procedures when you're terminally ill or when you have no prospect for recovering from a serious illness. In your living will, you may give certain health-care directives and name an agent to make medical decisions on your behalf if you're unable to make these decisions yourself. This designation of a health-care agent is often done in a separate health-care power of attorney. Some states allow you to include these two most important documents—the living will and the health-care power of attorney—in one complete document. This helps eliminate the possibility of confusing the terminology in the two documents, which would lead to improper decisions. I recommend, where possible, to combine these two documents.

The Value of Having a Living Will

The importance of having a living will was dramatically emphasized by the 2005 saga of Terri Schiavo in Florida. She was kept on artificial life support for more than 11 years—even after the Florida courts had repeatedly found, based on reliable medical testimony, that she was in a permanent, vegetative state with no possibility of recovery. The Florida legislature, Florida governor, the United States Supreme Court, the United States Congress, and the federal courts all became involved in the case. They systematically tried to overrule the husband's request that Terri be allowed to die a natural death, without the use of extraneous heroic measures to extend the dying process.

Whatever happened to the separation of powers created by our United States Constitution? No matter where you stand on this issue, wouldn't you agree that Terri should have been able to express her own wishes in this matter? Years of court cases and family heartache could have been avoided if Terri Schaivo had executed a valid living will in writing before her injury.

Your right to decide not to be kept artificially alive was emphasized by the U.S. Supreme Court in its decision regarding Nancy Cruzan years ago. However, to make sure your wishes are carried out, you should express them in writing. That's the lesson Terri Schiavo taught us.

Most people who sign a living will want to avoid being kept alive by technology in a vegetative state or simply being kept alive by technology to prolong the dying process. My office provides a wallet-sized living will—a standard living will document encased in a plastic sleeve. Popular with my clients, this wallet-sized living will (the size of a credit card) is designed to be kept in your wallet, purse, or the glove compartment of your car. It's important to have it available in the event of an emergency.

Minor Child Considered "Incapacitated" in the Law

If you have children who are minors, they don't have the legal capacity to enter into a legally binding contract. They must have an adult look after their interests. As far as the law is concerned, they're incapacitated. You should name someone to act on behalf of any minor or incapacitated children in your will or trust.

As with poor Mrs. Banks, being judged incapacitated can be devastating. That's why it's critical to realize that, under the law, a minor child is considered an incapacitated person. Many unexpected problems can arise in a minor's conservatorship. Let me share a story that highlights this issue.

Mr. Jones, one of my trust clients, was reviewing his newly signed trust documents at home. His 14-year-old daughter, Wanda, came into his study as he was doing so. She asked what he was doing. Mr. Jones briefly outlined the trust and its benefits. He explained that if he were to die, his estate would belong to her—his only child. Mr. Jones also noted that he had provided in the trust for his brother, Wanda's uncle, to supervise the trust funds until she reached the age of 25. If something were to happen to Mr. Jones before Wanda turned 25, her uncle was to make money available to pay for her education and general living expenses. Because Mr. Jones had established a trust, his estate wouldn't be held up in the probate court and Wanda's uncle wouldn't be required to report each expenditure to the judge.

When Wanda returned home to her mother's custody (Mr. and Mrs. Jones were divorced), she reported to her mom what her dad had done, trying to explain the advantages of a trust. Mrs. Jones replied that she'd been planning to do the exact same thing.

The next week, tragedy struck. Mrs. Jones was killed in a plane crash. Her plans to establish a trust had not materialized … and never would. As the natural father, Mr. Jones became Wanda's guardian. Wanda inherited her mother's estate.

Mrs. Jones never created a revocable living trust, which caused unexpected problems for her ex-husband. In the first year after Mrs. Jones's death, the probate court required Mr. Jones to appear before the judge on three occasions to render an accounting for Wanda's inheritance. These appearances had nothing to do with the probate; they were merely to provide a status report on the funds that Wanda had already inherited. The court had placed all of Wanda's funds in restricted or bonded accounts. Mr. Jones couldn't make independent decisions on behalf of his daughter and her inheritance. Yet each time he was asked to appear in court, Mr. Jones had to take off time from work. After each hearing, the judge "took the matter under advisement" and didn't render a decision until weeks later.

Finally, several years (and several thousand dollars in legal fees) later, Wanda received her mother's estate. Mr. Jones recently admitted that he wished he had tried harder to influence his ex-wife to complete her revocable living trust. The court released Wanda's trust funds to her when she reached the age of 18. Concerned about a sporty, red convertible she was eying, Mr. Jones knew she wasn't mature enough to handle her newfound "wealth." And for good reason: That became her first purchase after her inheritance. However, Wanda wasn't totally immature. Her father suggested she meet with me. I helped her establish plans for her future and we discussed the wise use of her inheritance. It was interesting that one of Wanda's first acts was to establish her own revocable living trust. Then she took a trip to Europe!

In contrast, Mr. and Mrs. Jacobs carefully planned the distribution of their estate. With the help of an attorney, they placed their assets and life-insurance proceeds in a revocable living trust for their six minor children. They named Mrs. Jacobs's brother and his brother's wife as guardians of the children. They named Mr. Jacobs's brother as trustee. His duty was to manage the funds for the benefit of the six children until each reached the age of 30. The trust provided for the children's maintenance, housing, education, medical costs, and other living expenses.

Several years later, while flying a private plane, Mr. and Mrs. Jacobs's plane crashed. Both died. As directed in the trust, the six orphans went to live with their paternal aunt and uncle. Six children! Because the size of their family increased suddenly and dramatically, the foster parents were able to use trust funds to purchase and remodel a larger home to accommodate everyone. The estate—and much needed funds—weren't held up in the courts.

As the Jacobs's children have matured, they've begun to realize the significant benefits their parents provided for them through careful planning. Although nothing could bring their parents back, the children's lives were not nearly as disrupted as they might have been.

Using a Trust with a Professional Corporation

Licensed professionals have a specific reason for establishing a revocable living trust and naming themselves as grantors and sole trustees. Doctors, lawyers, accountants, and other professionals who own their own professional corporations can set up their trusts to satisfy all legal requirements and still avoid probate in the event of their deaths.

The stock in a professional corporation must be owned by the individual with the professional license, for example, the doctor, the lawyer, or the orthodontist. The law makes an allowance for the "professional corporation trust" to hold the stock owned by the licensed professional in the professional corporation. The professional corporation trust is simply a revocable living trust with a specific purpose: to keep a licensed individual's interest in a professional corporation out of probate in the event of the death of its owner. This trust has certain restrictions. The successor trustee may administer the trust to sell its asset—the stock in the professional corporation—but not to practice the specific profession (e.g., medicine, law, or dentistry).

With this planning, a business won't be subject to a dramatic loss in value upon the death of the professional. Should the grantor meet an untimely demise, a successor trustee can have the authority to immediately liquidate the corporate assets or sell the ongoing business. In this way, the professional practice won't be too badly disrupted—as it most certainly would be if the practice had to go through probate. The monetary value of the practice can remain basically intact.

Another true story may offer the best explanation. An orthodontist established a revocable living trust and named a successor trustee. This planning greatly benefited his family. When he died unexpectedly of a heart attack, his wife became trustee of the stock in his professional corporation. As anticipated in the trust, she was able to sell the ongoing practice within two weeks after her husband's death. If the orthodontist's practice had gone into probate, the practice could have quickly lost half its value— or more—for one simple reason: If the dentist isn't there when the patients need their braces adjusted, the patients, out of necessity, will take their business elsewhere.

Problems in Joint Tenancy, Right of Survivorship, and Community Property

Revocable living trusts can remedy problems that are inherent with joint tenancy of property, right of survivorship, and community property. Although some people use joint tenancy to avoid probate, the problems associated with wills and the probate process can still catch up with them.

If you own real estate, you may be familiar with joint tenancy property. Deeds for married couples show the owners as: "John Doe and Jane Doe, as husband and wife, as joint tenants with right of survivorship and not as tenants in common and not as community property." This means that in the event of the death of either person listed on the document, the property automatically passes to the survivor. No probate is involved. That's the upside to what's known as *right of survivorship*. It eliminates probate on the death of the first spouse. In those instances, in the event of the death of either spouse, it's better to own property in joint tenancy with right of survivorship than to have that property become subject to a will and therefore pass through a probate process.

However, property in joint tenancy doesn't avoid probate in these two events: a common disaster in which both parties are killed or after the death of the second spouse. In both cases, the assets must go through probate.

Depending on joint tenancy to eradicate any possible probate problems can lead to serious trouble. Let me introduce you to Mrs. Tenancy. She came to see me after the death of her husband because she wanted help on the distribution of his property.

A few days earlier, Mrs. Tenancy had gone to her bank to withdraw one of her certificates of deposit in the name of both her and her husband. The bank officer stated, "Since your husband has died, we can't release these funds to you without a court order."

Although the account was in both their names, it didn't specify right of survivorship. That's the first problem with joint tenancy: The belief that the right of survivorship exists just because both names are present on the document; the ownership must actually indicate a right of survivorship.

Because other banks had already complied with her request, Mrs. Tenancy was confused … and that's why she came to see me. As I looked over her documents, I was happy to give her good news. Since her certificate of deposit was for a sum less than $15,000, it could be transferred to her by affidavit. She wouldn't have to go through a full probate; this process would be quick and inexpensive.

Next, she brought out three deeds to her residence. The first deed showed that she and her husband had owned the property as joint tenants with right of survivorship. It sounded good. However, in 1981, they had transferred the property out of their names to a third party and then back into their names. (This is called a *straw-man transfer* and is often used to create a new or different type of property ownership.) Unfortunately, they transferred the property back as community property.

Mrs. Tenancy didn't remember much about the transfer. She only knew that, in 1981, she and her husband became involved in an investment they thought might increase the size of their estate. To reduce capital gains taxes on a future sale, their attorney had recommended they take their property out of joint tenancy and title it as community property. The couple hadn't realized that community property doesn't avoid probate. The attorney should have recommended they use a revocable living trust. (Currently, a new method to hold title is available: community property with right of survivorship. But this wasn't available at the time.)

It's uncomfortable to tell a widow that her recently deceased husband's estate now owned half of her residence. We had to probate this estate to transfer half of the residence to her, the only heir of the estate. I was glad for

Mrs. Tenancy that her case took the shortest amount of time I'd experienced to complete a probate: only five and a half months.

Mrs. Tenancy came back to see me after the probate process was completed. She was determined that, upon her death, all her assets could be distributed to her children without having to go through probate. She wisely transferred all her assets to her own revocable living trust.

I recommend you never hold title to any property in joint tenancy with right of survivorship with anyone other than your spouse. Remember, once you place property in joint tenancy, both parties are considered owners of that property. This means the property is now subject to the debts and liabilities of either party. Generally, this isn't a problem if you are husband and wife; you usually have the same debts and obligations anyway. But if you share joint tenancy with someone other than your spouse, this can cause serious problems.

The Issue of Ownership

Picture this: A widow asked me to help her retitle her home and another house that she owned in which her son's family was living. She wanted the ownership of both houses to be transferred to her one son upon her death without going through the probate process. She thought joint tenancy with right of survivorship would be the easiest and least expensive way to accomplish this.

I knew I would advise her against joint tenancy, but I didn't want to blurt out my disapproval when she seemed set on that approach. So I asked her to tell me about her son. This client, Mrs. Widow, seemed eager to discuss him with me. Edgar was a middle-aged man, married to a woman she didn't care for. They had several young children. At the present time, Edgar was working in a department store but he was about to leave that job. He had just fallen into a promising opportunity to open his own restaurant and he wanted to take advantage of it.

"Well," I interjected. "Let's just take a look at what might happen if you put your property in joint tenancy with your son. Not that it will happen, but let's see what could happen. Let's assume your son leaves his job and becomes involved in the restaurant business. To do that, he'll sign a long-term lease on a property he locates that he believes will be the perfect location for his clientele. He'll probably purchase a walk-in refrigerator, a large range and oven, pots and pans, menus, dishware, and an inventory of food and supplies. And he'll have to hire help. Let's assume he sinks his life savings into his new venture. Then, about three or four months later, he finds out that he chose the wrong location for this kind of a restaurant. The business fails.

"He still owes people a lot of money. They're anxious to be paid, but he can't pay them because he's already spent his life savings trying to start the restaurant. His creditors file a lawsuit against him and get a judgment. Wanting their judgment satisfied, his creditors search the county records and immediately find that he's the joint owner of the house in which he lives. Plus, he's the joint owner of his mother's house. They can execute their judgment against both pieces of property. The court may order you to sell your home and his to pay the judgment. You could end up losing your home because of your decision to use joint tenancy." I could see doubt beginning to show in Mrs. Widow's eyes.

I continued, "But that probably won't happen to you. Your son will be successful in the restaurant business and you won't have to worry about that. Let's assume he is successful. In fact, he has a good business. He's so happy about his thriving business that one day, before he goes home, he takes an extra drink. He gets in his car and on the way home, he's involved in a terrible car accident. Several people are killed. The police test his blood-alcohol level at the scene and it's over the legal limit. The accident is his fault! The families of those killed in the accident sue him to pay for their losses. They win the lawsuit and the court awards them a judgment. Your son doesn't have enough insurance to cover all the liability, but the families of the people who were killed in the accident need to be paid. They want the money the court said they're entitled to. Even selling his business doesn't cover the debt. The plaintiff's attorneys search the county records and find that your son isn't only the joint owner of the home in which he's residing—he's also the joint owner of his mother's home. *Your* home, Mrs. Widow. They can execute their judgment against both properties. You could lose your home over your son's automobile accident." At this point, Mrs. Widow's eyes aren't merely registering doubt, they have opened wide in concern.

I proceeded in a calm voice. "Now, this probably won't happen because, of course, your son doesn't drink. In any event, his insurance will be sufficient to cover any damages resulting from an automobile accident. But, let's assume his business is successful, he doesn't drink, and he's careful to maintain adequate auto insurance. In fact, his business is doing so well, he hires a business manager to take care of his books and pay the bills. The business manager neglects to pay the quarterly taxes on time or file the proper reports. We all know the IRS likes to be paid. The IRS wants immediate recovery of its money. IRS lawyers can file a notice of levy or a tax lien. That notice applies to any property on which your son's name appears. And, thanks to joint tenancy, this includes his home and your home, Mrs. Widow. The IRS doesn't care how they get paid. They just want payment. They could take *both* properties to satisfy the tax lien. Yes, you could lose your home because your son didn't pay his taxes."

Mrs. Widow leaned slightly forward in her chair. She seemed eager to hear one more reason why a joint tenancy could be disastrous for her.

Again I replied that none of these occurrences were likely in her case. But I felt I needed to make an additional comment about this potential situation. Mrs. Widow had already declared that she didn't have much use for her daughter-in-law. So I threw a little more wood on the fire. I asked whether her son's marriage was stable; she didn't think it was. I asked her to envision what could happen if a divorce were to occur. She noted that the daughter-in-law could claim an interest in her husband's home, as well as her own home, since her husband's name appeared on both deeds. Her home was at risk because of her son's insecure marriage.

Mrs. Widow declared that she would have none of that!

I agreed and added that the couple could get counseling with goal of stabilizing their relationship—and their marriage.

I was certain I'd already convinced her that joint tenancy wasn't a good option, but I continued in my dissertation on disaster. "Let's assume none of these problems happens to you. Your son does well in his business. He doesn't drink and isn't involved in an automobile accident. In any event, he retains excellent automobile accident and liability insurance coverage. He supervises his business carefully and pays all taxes in a timely fashion. His marriage is improving. Everything is going quite well.

"One day you decide your home is too much work for you. The yard maintenance is a headache and the house needs paint. You decide you would be more comfortable in a retirement community. You locate a friendly retirement haven that maintains the exterior of each residence, provides all lawn care, and even provides activities and meals. You tender a down payment on the new place and list your home for sale.

"You find a buyer for your home and agree to all the terms. You appear at the escrow office to sign the final sales documents. The title officer asks about the second person listed as owner on the deed to your home. You explain that this person is your son. The title officer says your son must also sign the deed to complete the transaction.

"So you tell your son that he must sign the deed to complete the sale. You're shocked by his response, 'Well, Mom, we like having you live just down the street. You're handy when we need a sitter for the kids. We can keep our eye on you. If you're worried about your yard, I'll mow the grass and trim the shrubs. I'll even paint the eaves for you. I don't want you to move. I'm not going to sign the deed.'" I leaned forward and asked, "Mrs. Widow, do you know that you wouldn't be able to sell your home without your son's approval?"

The room exploded in silence as Mrs. Widow licked her lips and replied, "You paint a frightening picture, Mr. Allen. I don't want my son's name on my deed—no matter what! But I still don't want my son to have to suffer through the probate process upon my death. What do you recommend?"

Deeply relieved, I suggested she set up a simple revocable living trust and transfer all her property into it. She agreed. She transferred her home and her son's home into that trust. She also included her stocks, bonds, investments, certificates of deposit, and personal property in her trust. She named herself the trustee. She named her son to act as the successor trustee in the event of her death or incapacity. Her son was also the only beneficiary. Upon her death, both properties and all other assets in her trust will transfer to her son without going through probate.

And, of great importance to Mrs. Widow, during her lifetime, neither property is subject to her son's debts or liabilities. If he isn't successful in the restaurant business, Mrs. Widow won't lose her home. If he's in a car accident without sufficient insurance or doesn't file his taxes on time, she won't have to worry about her son's creditors or the IRS. She doesn't need to get her son's approval if she decides to sell her home. She's in full control of her trust. Mrs. Widow emphasized the other benefit: "I don't have to worry that my son's wife might divorce him and claim an interest in the home I've provided for them. Or even in my own home."

Last summer, Mrs. Widow came to see me again. She had recently remarried and wanted to know what effect that might have on the trust we had established. I explained that since she was a widow when she had set up her trust, all her property was considered her sole and separate property. It remained sole and separate property in her trust. Her new husband had no claim to any of it. She didn't have him sign a premarital agreement—and wouldn't have needed him to sign one. Mrs. Widow was happy to learn this. She hadn't wanted to ask him to sign, as she put it, an "agreement to get a divorce."

The examples I cited to Mrs. Widow about joint tenancy aren't jokes. I can't stress this fact enough: Never hold joint tenancy with anyone other than your spouse.

Unfortunately, another client learned this the hard way. While I was helping Mrs. Goodson gather the documentation necessary to complete her revocable living trust, I noticed that the deed to her home listed her son as a joint tenant. I asked, "Mrs. Goodson, did you realize that you son's name is on the deed to your home?"

She replied, "Oh, yes. When my husband died, my lawyer recommended that I put the home in joint tenancy with right of survivorship with my son."

I explained, "In order to put your home into your trust, your son will have to sign on a transfer deed to the trust."

"No problem," she confidently responded. "He's my favorite and most dependable son."

When her revocable living trust was ready to sign, I asked her to bring her son to our meeting so I could explain to him the terms and advantages of her trust and ask him to sign the deed transferring her home into the trust. We read through the trust together. Mrs. Goodson signed her trust, her Last Will and Testament (often referred to as *a pour-over will*), other transfer notices, and the deed to her home. After she signed her deed, she passed it to her son for his signature.

The son studied the deed for a few moments before he acknowledged her request. "Mother, I understand your home is now in joint tenancy with right of survivorship. And if you should die, the home becomes mine because of this right of survivorship. Isn't that correct?"

She answered that he was correct and I agreed. "Well," he said, "I like it that way. I don't think I want to change it. I'm not going to sign that deed." Mrs. Goodson's face registered shock and surprise. She recovered her composure enough to finish our conference. We completed the trust and other transfers. However, because her son refused to sign the deed, we left her home out of her trust.

As you might guess, Mrs. Goodson soon changed the beneficiaries of her trust. The-unwilling-to-sign-the-deed son is no longer a beneficiary. He'll receive the home upon her death, but he won't share the balance of the estate with her other children. He would have been better off sharing in the whole estate rather than just the home. Remember, never own any property in joint tenancy with anyone other than your spouse—not even with your favorite son!

Be Careful of Joint Tenancy

Even with a spouse, you need to be careful of joint tenancy. Interesting problems can arise and it's good to consider several possibilities. For example, you could unintentionally disinherit someone, as in the following tragic story.

A young married couple with young children held everything they owned in joint tenancy with right of survivorship. The wife died unexpectedly, leaving everything to the husband. There was no probate and all the property now belonged solely to the husband. Later, the husband met a woman who was divorced and had children from her prior marriage. The widower and the divorcee married. They retitled all of their property together in joint tenancy with right of survivorship.

Unfortunately, this new couple was involved in an automobile accident. The husband died immediately. The wife survived, but had to stay in the hospital for several months. As the survivor, all of the couple's property went to the second wife by her right of survivorship. After months in the hospital, she died of complications from the injuries sustained in the car accident. All of the couple's property went to her children by her previous marriage. Nothing went to her stepchildren— the children of the first wife. No one intended this to happen, but it did due to the way they had titled the property. Because of the joint tenancy with right of survivorship, the husband's children by his first marriage were disinherited.

People ask me, "Can't we initially put everything in joint tenancy with right of survivorship? Then if something happens to one of us, we could put everything into a trust at that time and still avoid probate on the second death?" My response is, "Of course you can—but who can guarantee that you'll have the opportunity?" The woman in the hospital had wanted to take care of her husband's children by his previous marriage. But the auto accident left her incapacitated and she was unable to make the necessary change. As a result, when her husband died, his children were disinherited.

Do your estate planning now—while you're still able. Don't wait, hoping that you'll never experience similar problems!

Revocable Living Trust and Your Estate Plan

A revocable living trust should be the foundation of any estate plan. If you're married and your estate is valued at more than the applicable exclusion amount (or is likely to grow in value to this amount), I recommend you have a revocable living trust with an A/B trust election.

Keep in mind that not all revocable living trusts are created equal. I've observed that many living trust plans—even some created by lawyers—don't include everything that's necessary. Some don't even transfer assets into the trust, thus leaving the assets subject to probate. (The assets will eventually become a part of the living trust through the pour-over will, but only after probate.) This eliminates one of the main benefits of the living trust: avoiding probate altogether.

After many experiences, both good and bad, I've learned how important it is to create, generate, and produce living trust plans that are complete. A good plan must include a living will and power of attorney. A good plan must also be fully funded so your estate won't be subject to probate.

A complete estate plan will include:

1. Living trust document (with A/B trust election for a married couple, if needed)
2. Backup pour-over will
3. Schedule of trust assets
4. Assignment of personal property
5. Deeds to transfer real estate (including your residence)
6. Documents for the transfer of assets to your revocable living trust
7. Guidelines for trustee
8. Letter to successor trustee
9. Instructions on how to keep your trust current
10. General durable power of attorney
11. Living will and medical power of attorney
12. Glossary of legal terms
13. Notary and witness service
14. A trust binder and organizer

Be sure to keep your revocable living trust updated. Purchase any new property and automobiles in the name of your trust. I recommend you review your trust assets annually, either with your spouse, by yourself, or with your attorney.

///

Action Items—Chapter 4: "Trust Me..."

Take a moment to complete the following action items and keep reading to learn more on the benefits of a revocable living trust.

Action 1: Who will care for your children?—If you have children, do the directions in your estate plan clearly describe how your children are to be cared for in case you and your spouse die? If not, take immediate steps to identify a guardian and develop guidelines for an efficient, controlled inheritance.

Action 2: Review the titles to your properties—Do you share joint tenancy of property with anyone other than your spouse? Do you have property listed as community property that doesn't include the right of survivorship? If so, I encourage you to immediately change the deed, if possible, to solely control the property.

Action 3: Do you have a living will and medical power of attorney?—If not, set this up soon! Don't wait, even if you're young and healthy. Unfortunately, accidents can happen to anyone. Most attorneys (and even many hospitals) have a generic form for a living will and the appointment of a health-care agent. If you're in an accident or a medical emergency arises and you must be admitted to a hospital, the hospital is now required to ask if you have a living will. But what good is that living will if you answer *yes*, but you don't have it with you? It's helpful to have a living will that's small enough to keep in your purse or wallet. Then if there's an emergency, you'll have your living will with you and the hospital can make a copy of it for its files. You can take action right now! Visit *www.PocketLivingWill.com* to order your pocket-size living will.

Action 4: If you have a trust, is it complete and in order?—Review your trust documents to ensure you have a complete set of documents including a schedule of assets, assignment of personal property, and deeds to transfer real estate. If you're married, check to see if you have an A/B provision. If not, ask your attorney to revise your revocable living trust to include this. Finally, take time to update your trust to reflect your current properties, automobiles, and investments.

Action 5: Make certain your documents include HIPAA language where required—If you haven't updated your trust, power of attorney, living will, and health-care power of attorney since 2002, they probably don't contain the proper language required to comply with the current law (formally known as the Health Insurance Portability and Accountability Act or HIPAA). This language is required to authorize your doctor to release any and all individually identifiable health information and any other medical records to your successor trustee or health-care agent.

Go to *www.EstatePlanningDr.com/book* to download:

Outline of Guardianship Information—(including directions for children's care and guidelines for receiving their inheritance.)

Deed Analysis Form

Trust Checklist

Chapter Five

Twelve Costly Misconceptions About Wills

I've worked in estate planning for more than 30 years and have heard a smorgasbord of questions on the subject of estate planning. Many queries are amazingly off the wall. However, most people ask the same few questions. Twelve common—and costly—misconceptions about wills follow. Even though I've addressed some of these misconceptions in previous chapters, they're worth reviewing as a group here.

Misconception One: Probate Costs are Low

The idea that probate costs are low is a common misconception—and it's not true! The average cost to settle an estate is $5,000 to $10,000 and often it's much more than that.

Many people ask if it's possible to handle a probate without using a lawyer. The answer is *yes*. The law doesn't require you to hire an attorney. However, probate can become complicated. In the Arizona law books, for example, the portion relating to the transfer of property upon death consists of 444 pages! Most people don't have the time or inclination to read 444 pages of legal jargon to handle their own probate problems. And, unfortunately, the courts aren't helpful when individuals try to handle probates on their own. In fact, courthouse workers aren't allowed to offer legal assistance. Even if they want to explain your filing dates and other requirements, the law specifies that they aren't allowed to do so. Probating a will becomes a difficult process for most people.

Several clients have approached me with the same sad tale of woe, "We started to handle the probate of a relative who died. We finally just threw up our hands. We need help with this!" That's when they find an attorney to finish the process.

Misconception Two: A Will or Testamentary Trust Avoids Probate

No, neither a will nor a testamentary trust avoids probate. A will is a unique document. It has absolutely no legal affect until the death of the person who signed it. Because of this factor, it must go through the probate process to be effective.

A testamentary trust is simply a trust that's a part of a will, so it, too, is subject to probate. When a testamentary trust is involved, the trustee must report to the courts annually (and sometimes more often) as long as the trust exists.

A client once commented that he wasn't concerned about probate because an attorney had set up a trust for him several years earlier. I asked him a few questions and it became clear that his trust was simply a testamentary trust, meaning it was a part of his will. When I informed him that his testamentary trust wouldn't offer him freedom from probate, he was surprised and mystified why the other attorney hadn't told him this. This client was determined to avoid the probate process so we set up a revocable living trust. Remember, a testamentary trust doesn't avoid probate.

Misconception Three: You Can Handle Permanent and Vacation Homes Through the Same Probate

Yes, both your permanent home and vacation home can be handled through the same probate—if both properties are located in the same state. But if you own property in more than one state, each state requires a probate to transfer the title to the heirs. Remember Mrs. Will who had owned property in both Arizona and Colorado? Her estate had to undergo a second probate because she had owned property in a second state. Many "snowbirds" from northern states move to Arizona to enjoy the pleasant winter weather and maintain property in two states. Upon their deaths, their estates must conduct probates in both states—unless they avoid this by using simple revocable living trusts. These people can transfer property from more than one state to their revocable living trusts, thus eliminating a probate in each state. For those who own property in more than one state, a revocable living trust is the wisest way to own title.

Misconception Four: A Will Can Be Probated in Only a Few Weeks

No, the courts can't probate a will in only a few weeks. In fact, state laws require from three to six months as a minimum time for a probate to be open and give creditors time to file claims against the estate. In Arizona, the law requires at least four months. On average, a probate takes between ten months and two years.

Misconception Five: In Probate, Your Will and Assets Remain Private

This misconception receives an emphatic *no!* Once a will is filed with the court, its contents become a matter of public record. Anybody has an opportunity to review those documents. Remember what happened when Natalie Wood died? Her 29 fur coats and $6,000,000 estate were the subject of an article in *The Wall Street Journal*. Simply stated, a will equals public record. In contrast, a revocable living trust remains a private family settlement. You decide which one is best for your family.

Misconception Six: Having a Will Helps You Avoid Taxes

No, a will by itself doesn't affect taxes in any manner. However, a revocable living trust can help seriously minimize estate taxes.

It's pathetic that one of the costs of dying is having to pay an estate tax. (Remember this old truism? *There are two things you can't avoid—death and paying taxes.*) Thankfully, a trust minimizes the fees and costs of settling your estate and also minimizes the taxes. Everyone currently enjoys a $2 million estate tax exemption; if the total value of your estate is less than that, your estate won't be taxed. If your estate is worth over $2 million (or you plan for it to be more than that), it's logical to assume that if you're married, together you can protect up to a $4 million from any estate taxes. But unless you do some planning, this won't be the case.

In the event of the death of a spouse, the law allows for an unlimited marital deduction. That means the estate isn't taxed if a person dies and leaves everything to the surviving spouse. This sounds great. However, if the second spouse has a will but no trust, upon the second spouse's death, all property is considered to be part of the estate of the second spouse, which can receive only one $2 million tax exemption. The net effect? Married couples who rely on wills but don't have trusts have only one federal estate tax exemption.

But you can protect yourself. With a little foresight and careful planning, you can claim that second $2 million estate tax exemption. You can transfer your property into your revocable living trust and stipulate that, in the event of the death of either spouse, the trust assets shall be divided into two trust shares known as Share A (survivor's share) and Share B (decedent's share). Each share retains the estate tax exemption. In addition to protecting up to $4 million from any estate taxes, you'll greatly reduce the taxes on anything over that amount.

Furthermore, many people don't realize that the money they receive from life insurance is included in the value of the estate when determining whether estate taxes are due. This is true even though insurance payments are made directly to the named beneficiary and don't go through probate. When you buy life insurance specifically to pay the estate tax, or when you purchase insurance to leave a cash payment to your family, it's a shame that the insurance payment is first reduced by a tax. You can completely avoid taxes on the insurance proceeds by setting up either a separate irrevocable life insurance trust (you'll learn more about this in Chapter Eight) or a properly structured family limited partnership. This trust or partnership actually owns your life insurance, removes the insurance from your taxable estate, and allows your estate to have the full benefit of the insurance.

Misconception Seven: A Will Prevents Quarrels over Assets

Wrong! As noted earlier, a will is the most contested of all legal documents. It's easy to contest a will. After all, a probate to administer the estate is already open. Anyone can file an additional pleading or request with the court. It's as simple as filing a document that might state, "Mom said she was going to change this provision just before she died" or "Dad was operating under the undue influence of my older brother when he made that provision" or "Both Mom and Dad were incapacitated when they signed their wills." Individuals could contest a will just to get an edge in the negotiating process. They hope everyone comes around to their way of thinking and settle the claim before the personal representative distributes the estate's assets.

In my years of estate planning, I've found nothing other than family good will prevents quarrels over estates. But, unlike a will, a trust is difficult to contest. First, trusts don't need to undergo a probate process so the court system isn't automatically involved. If a relative contests a trust, this person must start a new lawsuit and file a complaint showing that a good reason exists to set aside the trust. However, this is difficult to prove. Why? Because you set up the trust during your lifetime. You indicated by your use of the trust that you intended the trust's provisions to be in effect after your death. It would be difficult for your relative to say the trust isn't what you had intended. The courts rarely set aside the terms of a trust. Besides, a trust is usually settled relatively quickly, even before beneficiaries know how your property will be divided. It gives them nothing to argue about.

Misconception Eight: A Will from One State Isn't Legal in Another

This isn't true. If a will is valid in the state in which it was signed, it'll be valid in any other state. This issue was addressed in the United States Constitution: Every state must grant full faith and credit "to the public Acts, Records, and Judicial Proceedings of every other state." (Article IV, section 1). Be aware that even though your will is valid, it may be more difficult to administer an out-of-state will in the state where you reside at the time of your death.

In one case, a resident of Arizona died having a Pennsylvania will and owning real estate in Texas. To settle the estate, both the Texas and Arizona courts required that the Pennsylvania will be determined to be valid under Pennsylvania law. This requirement wasn't difficult in Arizona but proved to be a burden in Texas. If you move from one state to another and have a will from your previous state, consider taking time to review it and make sure it's up to date. You may be better off drawing up a new will. Rest assured, your will is a valid legal instrument as long as it's valid in the state in which it was drawn.

A trust will also be valid in every state. The bonus is that one trust may own property located in more than one state. In the example, wouldn't it have been better if the Arizona resident had set up a revocable living trust instead of relying on a will?

Misconception Nine: Drawing Up Your Will is the Only Cost of Planning Your Estate

This is absolutely not true! The cost of your estate plan is the total cost of settling your estate. If you choose to settle your estate with a will, you must include the cost of the probate process—whether that process costs $3,000 or $7,000 or $10,000. According to *Money* magazine, the average cost of settling an estate through probate is between 5 to 10 percent of the value of the estate. Therefore, the cost of settling a $200,000 estate averages $10,000 to $20,000.

Using a revocable living trust, you eliminate the most expensive part of estate settlement, the probate process.

Misconception Ten: To Raise Money, Family Members Can Liquidate Property Held by the Estate

The personal representative has the power to sell property in the estate but only for the purpose of paying all debts that the decedent's estate owes, not for the purpose of making a distribution to the family. The personal representative should not make any distributions from the probate estate until the final plan for distribution is prepared and approved, either by all the beneficiaries or by the court. If the personal representative makes a distribution before all the claims are settled—and the estate doesn't contain enough money to pay remaining claims—the personal representative is personally responsible for paying all the claims. That's why it isn't wise to make a distribution out of the estate until the court has approved a final plan.

A widow or widower's one-time allowance is exempt from this process. In Arizona, for example, the allowance is $18,000. If the surviving spouse needs more money than that, the spouse would go to court and show the judge that a good reason exists for an increase in the allowance. Of course, this process takes additional time and money so it's not a satisfactory procedure.

Misconception Eleven: In Your Will, You Must Name Your Attorney as Your Personal Representative

This isn't true! In most states, you may name anyone to act as your personal representative as long as the person designated is over 18. Your personal representative may even reside in another state. However, if you choose a corporation as your personal representative, some states require that it be a local corporation.

Some attorneys maintain that you must name your attorney as your personal representative. While that's patently untrue, these attorneys may argue their case: The attorney will handle the settlement of the estate. The personal representative, of course, is also entitled to a fee for the services provided. And the attorney for the personal representative is entitled to a fee. If the attorney acts as both the attorney and the personal representative, the attorney may feel entitled to a double fee.

A woman once came to see me about using a personal representative with a revocable living trust. Previously, another attorney had drawn up her will. After attending one of my seminars, she asked her attorney to change her will to a revocable living trust. Her attorney responded, "I don't know anything about revocable living trusts, but I'll give you a recommendation." He wrote down the name of another attorney. As she left his office, he added, "If you change your will, whatever you do, leave me in as your personal representative."

Well, she didn't! She hired me to prepare a new trust. Her previous attorney isn't included in the new will or the trust. In short, you don't have to name your attorney as your personal representative.

Misconception Twelve: Joint Tenancy is the Safest Way to Own Property

As you may remember from the previous discussion, this is a big mistake! Joint tenancy avoids probate when the first spouse in the joint tenancy dies. However, if both parties to the joint tenancy die in a common disaster or after the death of the second spouse, the jointly owned asset will still be subject to probate. Keep in mind that joint tenancy also means joint liability.

///

Action Items—Chapter 5: Twelve Costly Misconceptions About Wills

Take a moment to complete the following action items.

Action 1: Determine the value of your estate—If you have a will, estimate the current value of your estate. Now, how much is 5 percent of this amount? Ten percent? Add this to determine the actual cost to create your will. This represents the total cost to plan your estate. As your assets grow over the years, so will this amount.

Action 2: In which state was your current will established?—Do you have a will that was created while living in another state? If so, continue reading about trusts. Then make an appointment with an attorney in the state where you currently reside to set up a revocable living trust.

Action 3: Who is the personal representative of your estate?—Is your attorney named as your personal representative in your will or trust? If so, consider naming a new personal representative!

Chapter Six

Questions About Trusts

I once heard an attorney address a somewhat convoluted legal topic at a public seminar. At the end of his presentation a woman raised her hand and asked, "What do you charge?" The attorney responded, "I charge $150 for three questions." The lady responded, "That's quite a lot for just three questions, isn't it?" To which the attorney replied, "Yes, I suppose it is. What's your third question?"

The group chuckled and I'm sure she was tempted to ask a third question such as, "I'm not bothering you with all these questions, am I?"

The attorney could have replied, "Of course not. How do you expect to learn anything if you don't ask questions?"

I thoroughly agree—how can we learn anything if we don't ask questions? So this chapter is our question-and-answer period. Here are the top ten questions on the estate planning "hit parade." I hope this helps you learn more about wills and trusts—and I won't even charge you the three-question fee!

Common Questions About Revocable Living Trusts

Asking questions about revocable living trusts will help you become educated and, I hope, clear up any lingering hesitation you may have about trusts.

Here are the most common questions I hear in my practice and at the many seminars I present, with my answers.

Q. **I'm setting up a revocable living trust and want to transfer all my property (except for some personal items) into that trust. Will the personal items left out of the trust have to go through probate? Will there be a question about the value of those items or a problem with the transfer?**

A. When you set up a trust, you or your attorney should transfer all your titled property into your new trust. You should also include personal items in the transfer to the trust. This may be done with an "Assignment of Personal Property." This is a generic statement that includes language such as, "And miscellaneous items—personal belongings, household belongings, and furniture—located at the residence." Your revocable living trust should cover everything you have at your residence. Some people are specific when they itemize their list of property or trust assets. For practical reasons, no one will knock on your door and say, "Hey, you forgot to probate the tangible personal property of your deceased parents." If only tangible personal property is involved, you should have no problem.

Some types of personal property show ownership through legal title. This includes items such as automobiles, stocks, and even bank accounts. If you leave such personal property out of your trust and if this property has a value over the state exemption for probate (in Arizona, it's $50,000), this personal property must go through probate for the distribution to be effective. If the estate has creditors—or if titled personal property or real estate is involved—this almost always catches up to you. You'll need to clear the title to such property through a probate.

Q. How do you handle taxes through the trust?

A. The kind of trust most often used to avoid probate and reduce estate tax is called a revocable trust, an *inter vivos* trust, a living trust, a revocable living trust, or a grantor trust. All these different names or designations still mean revocable living trust. These trusts allow you to set up a trust during your own lifetime yet retain the right to alter, amend, or revoke any of the terms of that trust. Because you set up the trust in accordance with the law, for tax purposes, you're still considered the owner of all that trust property. Any income from your property, even if it's in trust, will be considered your income. File your tax return as you always have. Any income from the trust is reported as your income— even though it's in the name of the trust. You don't have to mention the trust. Your Social Security number remains the trust identification number. You don't have to get a separate identification number for the trust. The only difference is when you receive year-end interest or dividend reports from the bank or investment. These reports are in the name of your trust and show your Social Security number. Just include the reports with your personal income tax return. During your lifetime, there's no difference in trust income tax reporting.

Q. What if my successor trustee made some bad decisions and the trust no longer contained any property for my children?

A. This situation could cause a problem for your children. That's why it's critically important to choose a trustworthy successor trustee. Many people choose a bank; of course, bank representatives are covered by federal bank regulations. Even then, a bank may not be the best choice for successor trustee. Recently, a family recovered a multimillion dollar judgment against a large, local bank because the bank had dissipated the trust assets through unwise management.

In our case, my wife and I have chosen my daughter as successor trustee. We place a lot of faith and trust in her and believe she'll be a good manager. We've given her some guidelines of what we expect and hope she responds to that positively. The choice of successor trustee is a personal decision. The trustee is held to a higher standard of care than others because he operates on behalf of your beneficiaries. This is called a *fiduciary duty*. Successor trustees who violate their fiduciary duties are personally liable to the trust beneficiaries for any damages.

Q. **If both the husband and wife become incapacitated, how do you change control or regain control?**

A. The trust instrument itself usually covers that problem. The trust names the trust owners to act as trustees of their own trust until death, disability, legal incapacity, or resignation makes it impossible for them to continue. In the event that the original trustees are unable to serve for any of those reasons, the trust agreement names a successor trustee. The successor trustee manages the trust and all its assets upon the disability of the trustee. For example, if the trustee becomes incapacitated, the successor trustee must follow the instructions included in the trust agreement. The trust has a built-in mechanism to protect the trustee in the event of an incapacity. This eliminates the court procedure referred to as a *conservatorship*.

A well-written trust includes specific instructions for that eventuality. Furthermore, the successor trustee must get a letter from a physician verifying that the trustee is incapacitated and unable to handle the trust affairs. At that point, the successor trustee presents the doctor's letter or certification, together with the trust document, to the bank officer or the title company or whoever is responsible for managing the trust transaction. The successor trustee manages the property until its final distribution. If the original trustee recovers, then this trustee will be back in control. The transfer of control back to the original trustee is triggered by a new letter from the doctor indicating that the original trustee has recovered and may resume managing the trust assets and other affairs.

Q. Do we have any other supervision for our trust?

A. Take great care in choosing your successor trustee. Some people choose a professional corporation to serve in this capacity. Other than the successor trustee, no one except the trust beneficiaries supervise the management of the trust. After all, that's why it's called a *trust*. Some settlors will name successor co-trustees to add a degree of checks and balances.

Q. I want our children to receive portions of their inheritance at ages 25, 30, and 35. Does the revocable living trust document have a place for these instructions?

A. Yes, that information may be included in the original trust agreement. In fact, the trust is very flexible. If the settlors desire, the trust agreement may require an annual accounting to all the beneficiaries on the use of that trust until it's finally distributed to them. This safeguard exists so the beneficiaries can keep their fingers on the pulse and see what's happening with the property.

Q. If I have a trust set up, do I need a will, too?

A. Yes. When you set up a trust be sure and prepare a new Last Will and Testament—a pour-over will. This simple device communicates that upon your death if you have property outside of your trust, that property is "poured over" (transferred) to your trust for administration. This saves some of the problems in probate.

As an attorney, I hope my clients won't have to use a pour-over will. When the trust is established, all the property is transferred over to the trust so it'll avoid probate. The assets are re-titled in the name of the trust.

The pour-over will is a separate document that's a necessary part of your living trust plan. It revokes any prior will you may have executed and distributes your assets according to your plan in your living trust. Any property (real or personal) that you may have neglected to re-title in the name of your living trust will be transferred, or "poured-over," into your living trust by the pour-over will. However, if the total value of these items exceeds your state's probate exemption amount ($50,000 for Arizona), the pour-over will must go through the probate process to put assets into the trust. Therefore, it's important to keep your living trust updated—or funded by correctly titling your assets and keeping your schedule of trust assets up to date. Remember to re-title any property you purchase after setting up your revocable living trust. (For example, if you receive an

inheritance and forget to place it into an account or into
another asset held in the name of the trust.)

**Q. Who manages the transfer of the assets in my trust
when I die?**

A. When you establish your trust, you are the trustee or
trust manager. In your trust agreement, you name
someone to act as your back-up or successor trustee.
This person (or bank or trust company) will step into
your place as trustee upon your death. This successor
trustee will only need your original trust agreement
and a copy of your death certificate. This will allow the
successor to prove he is the proper designated person
to act as the current manager of your trust. No court
needs to be involved in this transfer of power. The successor trustee will then follow the instructions as you
have outlined them in your trust. You can see why it's
important to choose someone in whom you have faith
and confidence to carry out your designs. You want to
feel comfortable that the person you select is reason-
ably suited to follow your instructions.

**Q. What are the drawbacks of setting up a revocable liv-
ing trust?**

A. As trite as it sounds, it's difficult to name any significant drawbacks to a revocable living trust. These instru-
ments initially cost more to set up than a will. But you
simply need to look at the whole picture: What is the
total cost to settle your estate? You'll find that it costs
considerably less to use a trust.

A second possible drawback is that you must be disciplined. You must keep current the trust's list of trust assets (sometimes called *schedule of trust property*). As you buy, sell, or change real property and investments, you need to update your lists and schedules. The only real drawback is disciplining yourself to stay current.

I really have to look hard to find any other drawbacks to a trust. A minor drawback could occur with property lenders. Admittedly, banks and other lenders are occasionally short-sighted. If you're re-mortgaging your home, for example, or want a home equity credit line, the banks are sometimes reluctant to give you a loan unless the property is in your own name—not in the name of your trust.

I asked the vice president of a bank about this issue. His reply was deeply gratifying. "You know, I don't understand that either. I've worked in our bank trust department and as a bank vice president," he said. "Really, the bank is better protected by having the property in a trust because it avoids probate if that person dies. But for some reason, the loan officers or bank directors don't see this. They sometimes require that you actually transfer your property out of your trust and put it in your name until the loan is made. After that, they don't have any objection to you re-titling the property back into the name of the trust." This practice didn't make sense even to the bank vice president. Some people could consider this to be a possible drawback to the revocable living trust. But it's still a small price to pay for all the other benefits of a trust.

Q. Why do well-intentioned, responsible people put off planning their estate?

A. I believe this comes down to four major reasons: people feel intimidated by the legal process, they think the process will be too expensive, they don't want to face their own mortality, and—the most common and sometimes the most tragic reason—procrastination.

Reason 1: People are intimidated by lawyers and the legalities involved in estate planning—It's easy to overcome this problem by finding an attorney with whom you feel comfortable. Don't hesitate to ask your prospective attorney questions, even if you think they might seem silly. Don't feel bad because you don't understand the entire field of estate planning—that's why you pay an attorney. Also, choose an attorney with experience in the estate planning field. You need someone you can count on to handle all the legalities for you.

Reason 2: People believe that estate planning is too expensive—You can dispel this problem by thinking of estate planning as an investment, not an expense. Remember, the national average cost of probate is 5 to 10 percent of the value of the estate. If your estate is worth $300,000, the cost of probate would be $15,000 to $30,000. Think of it this way: Investing $2,500 to set up a living trust would avoid probate and may save as much as $25,000! A living trust is actually one of the most profitable investments you can make. I have never seen a probate that cost less to settle than a trust. Furthermore, if the estate is over $2 million in value, living trusts may save money on taxes. Although I'm a great proponent of patriotism, I don't want Uncle Sam, lawyers, and accountants to benefit from your life-long hard work.

Reason 3. People don't want to face their own mortality—Many people find it difficult to confront their own mortality. Let's face it, when people deal with estate planning, they're dealing with death. Some people have a vague superstition that if they face death, it'll happen. Well, the sad news is that if they *don't* face death, it'll still happen! Procrastinating on estate planning doesn't postpone death. Rest assured that no one has figured out how to accomplish effective estate planning after leaving this earth.

Instead of dwelling on estate planning as a death process, think of it as a life process. Proper estate planning ensures quality of life for your loved ones and peace of mind for you. Some real-life examples follow, illustrating why you shouldn't put off estate planning.

Widow Smith requested that I prepare a trust for her. Then, for some reason, she never came in to sign the deeds that needed to be transferred to her trust. I called several times encouraging her to come to my office to sign the deeds. But she kept putting it off. Ten years later, when her health was failing, Widow Smith's children called me to see if their mother's affairs were in order. I hated to tell them that, no, her affairs weren't in order. Unfortunately, before we could even start the process to redo the deeds and have her sign them, Widow Smith died. Her extensive properties all had to go through probate—all at great expense.

In another example, Mrs. Harris discussed with me the benefits of putting her assets in a trust and decided it was the wisest course of action. She intended to do so. Someone from my office called her every two weeks for several months. One day when someone in our office called Mrs. Harris, her son answered. Mrs. Harris had passed away a few days earlier.

Real-life Stories—Fictitious Names

"My father died more than four years ago. His estate is still going through probate. We still don't know what the total fees are yet, but we suspect they'll be close to $100,000. When I heard of the living trust, I set one up for my family right away. My children are now protected from having to go through all the hassles, unnecessary legal fees, and heartache that I've been through."

—Mrs. Willcott

"When my brother died, it took me 18 months to settle the estate and I couldn't believe what the attorney charged. My brother had a modest estate and only one heir."

—Mr. Davis

> "I am so thankful that my husband and I decided to prepare our estate plan when we did. Six months after we signed our trust, my husband had a stroke. A year later, he died. I never thought that I would lose him at our age. I guess you never know."
>
> —MRS. JOHNSON

> "We never thought about preparing an estate plan until my husband became mentally disabled due to an auto accident. The problem now is that, due to his disability, I can't make any decisions on his behalf without first consulting a judge. I can't prepare the documents needed to protect our family's future because my husband isn't competent to sign them. My hands are tied."
>
> —MRS. OWENS

Reason 4: People don't want to take the time—Almost every day in our office we hear, "Call me after my trip." "Call me after the holidays." "Call me after tax season." "Call me when I'm feeling better." Procrastination comes from the Latin root words *pro* (meaning *forward*) and *crastinus* (meaning *tomorrow*). It literally means: to put off until tomorrow. In English, it has come to mean: to put off intentionally or delay doing something that you should do. Procrastination, not ignorance, is the most common reason why people die without making any plans for their estate.

During my many years of experience in estate planning, I've witnessed firsthand the devastating results of procrastination; I relay some in the following examples.

Mr. and Mrs. Jackson attended an initial appointment to set up a trust. While our office was working on the trust papers, Mr. Jackson had a subacious hematoma, surgery, and then a stroke. We rushed the papers to the hospital. Fortunately, he was able to nod and make his mark—the papers were signed. Luckily, he had established his wishes before the stroke and the family could carry out his wishes as he desired.

Mr. and Mrs. Saunders attended one of my estate-planning seminars. They decided they needed to think about setting up a revocable living trust so they put off getting started. Shortly after the seminar, however, their options were suddenly and immeasurably restricted when Mr. Saunders had a heart attack and became incoherent. Mrs. Saunders doesn't know when, if ever, she will be able to create a trust.

Mr. Jenson, a client, called me with some deep concerns. He reported that a few weeks earlier his neighbor's wife, Mrs. Leonard had suddenly gone into a coma and had been taken to the hospital. After a month and a half, the doctors still couldn't find the cause. Mrs. Leonard's condition had worsened and her health continued to go downhill. She and her husband had not established a living will so she couldn't be taken off life support. The neighbors' financial resources were completely depleted by this tragedy. Because of this scare, Mr. Jenson called me to make sure everything was in order for him and his wife. It was.

I'm sharing these real-life examples from my law practice not to scare you or depress you, but to motivate you. The best time to stop procrastinating is now!

In his brilliant book *The Seven Habits of Highly Effective People*, Steven R. Covey explains the concept that certain actions or activities are important, though not urgent. Estate planning falls into that category. Urgent things demand your attention right now, this instant—such as a phone ringing or a dinner burning. Estate planning is important and becomes urgent only when a life-threatening event such as a heart attack or accident occurs. But then it may be too late. The process of estate planning isn't nearly as painful or time consuming as most people fear. As with any task that seems difficult or complicated, you must subdivide it into smaller, easier steps. (How do you eat an elephant? One bite at a time.)

What can you do right now to dispel these reasons for procrastination?

Do something today. Talk to your spouse. Organize your papers. Make any necessary phone calls. The estate planning process requires several weeks from initial consultation to signing. I implore you to start this important process today before it becomes urgent!

Ways of Using Revocable Living Trusts

Let's look at some positive examples of how people in different situations might use revocable living trusts.

Example 1: Mrs. Allred and her revocable living trust for a single person—Mrs. Allred is a widow with an estate worth a modest $100,000. She has no children and would like to leave her estate to her nephew without going through probate. Mrs. Allred creates a simple revocable living trust. She acts as trustee so she retains full control over her assets. In the event of her death or incapacity, she has named her nephew as successor trustee. Should she become incapacitated, her nephew could step in and manage her affairs until she recovers. He could do this without going to court.

Her neighbors recommended she place her assets in joint tenancy with her nephew. However, by wisely setting up a revocable living trust, Mrs. Allred has avoided the joint liability and other problems that could arise had she done this. She has retained control. More important, she has protected herself from involving the court should she become incapacitated—an important issue for her because she has no immediate family.

Because of the size of her estate, the estate won't owe taxes upon her death. Thanks to her revocable living trust, her estate won't be tied up in probate upon her death. She has saved approximately $7,500 in probate fees and costs and perhaps a similar amount by avoiding the need for conservatorship. (This figure is the average fee for such an estate—5 percent to 10 percent of the value of the estate—as noted by *Money* magazine in the article cited previously.) By planning her estate in this manner, she has also provided herself with peace of mind.

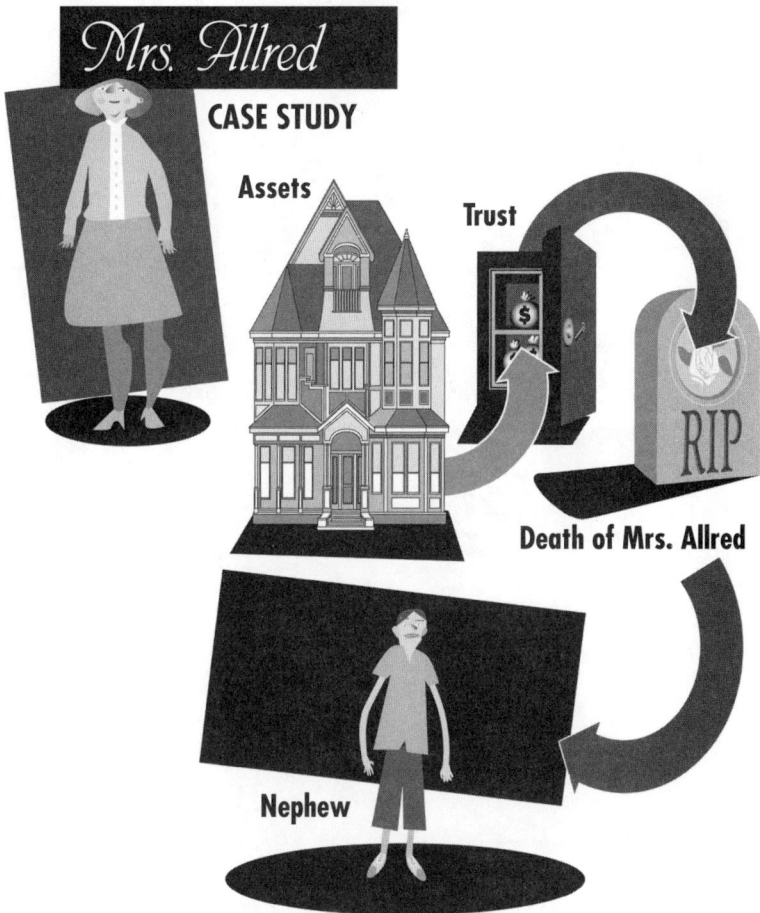

Mrs. Allred

CASE STUDY

Assets

Trust

Death of Mrs. Allred

Nephew

Example 2: Mr. and Mrs. Brown and their revocable living trust for a married couple—Mr. and Mrs. Brown's net worth is about $250,000. Their objective is to pass on their assets to their two grown children in equal shares but

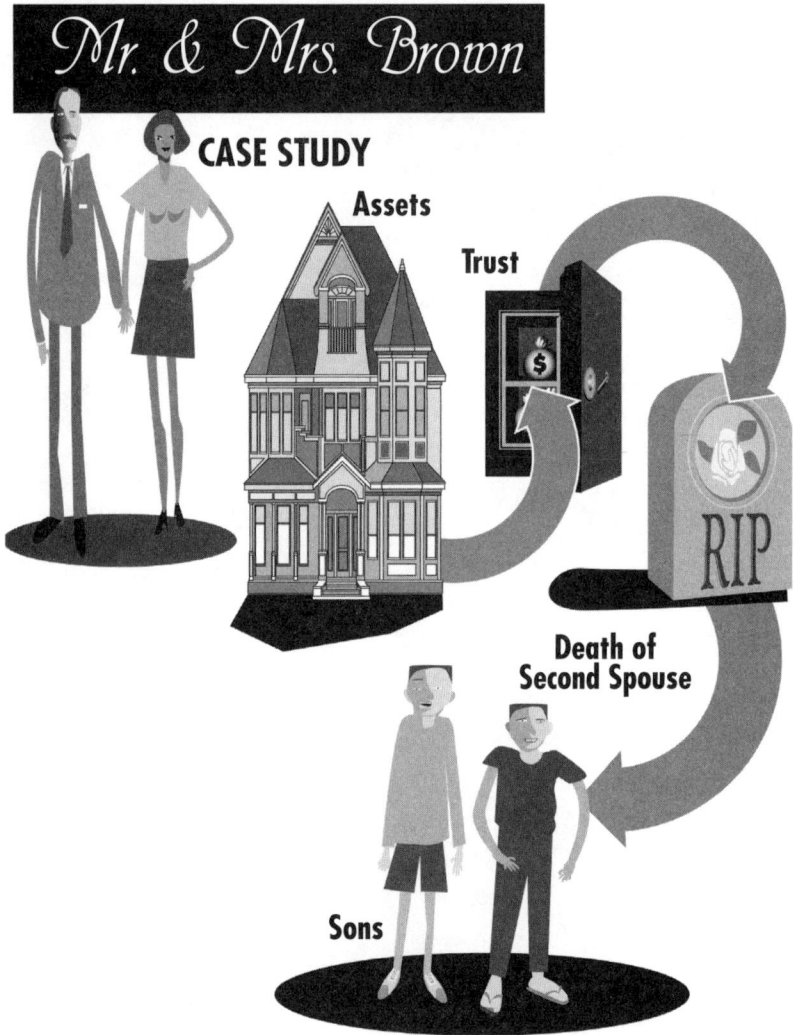

Mr. & Mrs. Brown

CASE STUDY

Assets

Trust

RIP

Death of Second Spouse

Sons

without probate. The Browns establish a simple revocable living trust, re-title the assets in the trust name, and are co-trustees. They select their oldest son as successor trustee upon their death or incapacity.

Upon the death of either Mr. or Mrs. Brown, the survivor will continue to have full use and control of the trust assets and income. Upon the death of both Mr. and Mrs. Brown, their assets will pass to their two children without probate. Because the estate is less than the $2 million tax exemption, their estate will pay no federal estate tax.

The use of a revocable living trust allows Mr. and Mrs. Brown to retain control over their assets during their lifetime. Because they appointed their son as successor trustee, they avoided conservatorship. If either Mr. or Mrs. Brown (or both) become incapacitated, the son could step in and manage their affairs until they recover. Because their children will inherit the Brown's estate without probate, they will save approximately $8,300 in costs and fees. (I arrived at this figure by using the State of California's approved probate fee for this size of an estate.)

Example 3: Mr. and Mrs. Clark and their revocable living trust for a married couple with a taxable estate— Mr. and Mrs. Clark wish to divide their estate among their four children in somewhat unequal shares and also without probate. Their assets are valued at more than $2 million so they want to protect the estate from owing taxes.

The Clarks set up an A/B Trust (also called a *marital deduction trust*). As you read earlier, when one spouse

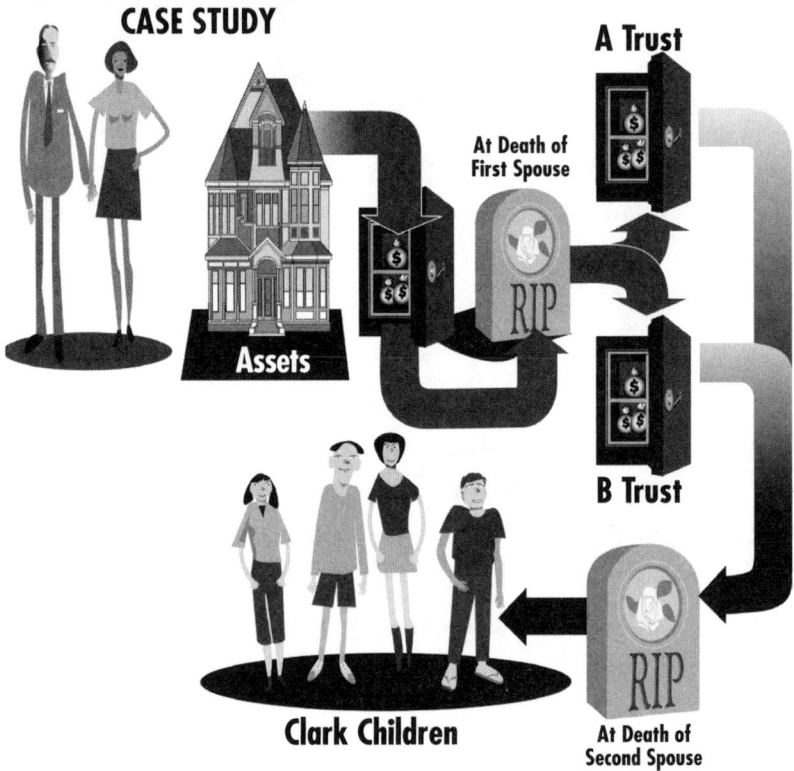

Mr. & Mrs. Clark

CASE STUDY

A Trust

At Death of
First Spouse

Assets

B Trust

Clark Children

At Death of
Second Spouse

dies, the trust assets are divided into two trust shares. Each share retains the current federal estate tax exemption. The surviving spouse will have full use of trust Share A. This spouse will also enjoy full use of the income from Share B, if needed, to maintain the current standard of living or provide for illness or accident. However, both trust shares retain the tax exemption so the Clark's estate can grow to as much as *$4 million* without owing a federal estate tax. Upon the death of both Mr. and Mrs. Clark, the estate will be passed to their children in the shares they described in their trust.

The Clarks will save at least $38,800 in federal estate taxes and an estimated $67,000 in probate fees and costs— a total savings to their estate of nearly $106,000 (These amounts are provided by the Federal Tax Tables and by California's statutory probate attorney fee schedule.) Like the Browns, the Clarks have retained control over their assets, avoided the need for a conservatorship in the event of incapacity, and saved on probate costs, fees, and taxes.

Example 4: Mr. and Mrs. Davis and their revocable living trust and irrevocable life insurance trust for a married couple with a larger taxable estate—Mr. and Mrs. Davis have money; they've accumulated an estate worth over $4 million and it continues to grow. What can they do to reduce the costs of taxes and other fees at the time of their death? First, they establish an A/B trust. This will protect up to $4 million from estate taxes, will avoid probate, and will allow them to control the distribution of their estate.

In addition, Mr. and Mrs. Davis create an irrevocable life insurance trust (ILIT). Note that a properly structured family limited partnership could create the same tax benefits. This trust purchased life insurance sufficient to pay any tax that would be due at the time of their death. Since the insurance policy is owned by the ILIT, the proceeds won't be taxed upon the death of Mr. or Mrs. Davis. The insurance proceeds are outside of the Davises' taxable estate. The Davis children are beneficiaries of this ILIT so they'll receive the proceeds and have liquid funds to pay any costs or taxes that might be due. The children won't be forced to sell any assets to pay these costs.

The estimated savings to the Davis estate by avoiding probate will be about $102,000, again following the California fee schedule. This savings is so substantial because no probate is required to settle the estate with a trust. In addition, the taxes saved by using the ILIT with the A/B trust, can amount to over $425,000 on a $1 million policy—or even more depending on the amount of insurance provided. Why such a large savings? Because the insurance proceeds paid to the ILIT are no longer included in the Davises' taxable estate for estate taxes. Without the ILIT, the tax on the insurance death benefit would have amounted to approximately 43 percent. In other words, the Davises have avoided having their estate pay more than $100,000 to attorneys and they've removed Uncle Sam as a "beneficiary" to their insurance policy, saving another $425,000. The $525,000, the total saved, will now go to their children—their real heirs.

Mr. and Mrs. Davis met their objectives of retaining control of their estate during their lifetime, protecting themselves in the event of incapacity, and passing on their estate to their children without going through probate.

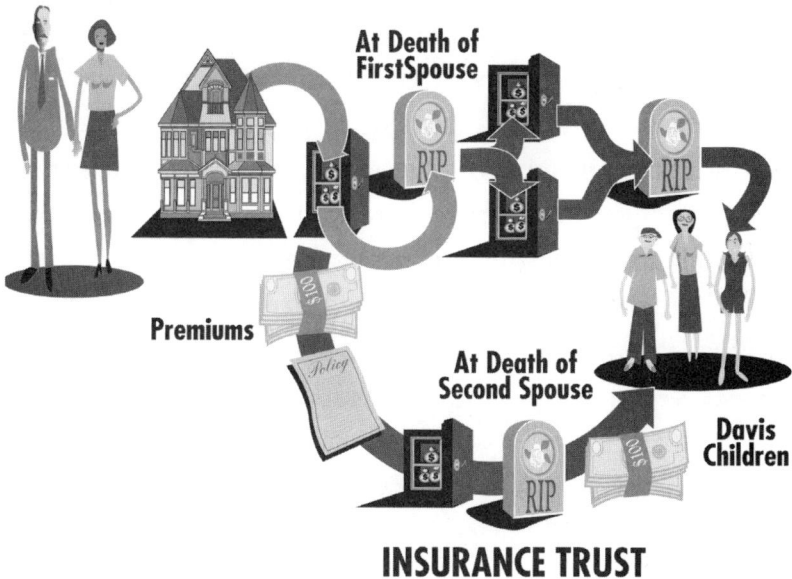

Mr. & Mrs. Davis
CASE STUDY

At Death of First Spouse

Premiums

At Death of Second Spouse

Davis Children

INSURANCE TRUST

Action Items—Chapter 6: Questions About Trusts

Take a moment to complete the following action items.

Action 1: Write down your questions about trusts— Do you have additional questions about revocable living trusts that aren't covered in this chapter? If so, write them down on a sheet of paper, and then continue reading this book. If the following chapters don't answer your questions, these would be great questions to ask an estate planning attorney.

Action 2: Have you been procrastinating on planning your estate?—First, let me congratulate you for reading this book. Right now, you're learning about estate planning and actively moving forward on this critical activity. Second, do you tend to procrastinate on estate planning? If so, why? Write down your reasons on a piece of paper. Consider these reasons, and then throw away that piece of paper! Promise yourself that you'll continue to pursue this immensely important activity.

Chapter Seven

It's Time to "Just Do It!"

You've read the reasons for setting up a revocable living trust. The evidence falls overwhelmingly in favor of revocable living trusts. You're committed to setting up a trust to protect yourself, your children, and your assets. Now what do you do?

First, list your assets. Some are obvious and include your home, automobiles, bank accounts, investments, IRAs, and insurance. Other assets are more subtle, especially personal property such as artwork, coin collections, and antique furniture. Estimate the value of all your assets; it may surprise you. Most people discover they're worth more than they thought. Determine if your estate is large enough to be subject to estate taxes upon your death.

Second, determine your objectives and write them down. Use the following questions to help you think about various objectives concerning planning your estate.

- What do you want to happen in the event of your death?

- Do you want everything to go to your spouse? To your children? To your church, or favorite charitable organization?
- Would you like to avoid probate?
- Do you want to eliminate any publicity regarding the settlement of your estate?
- Would you like to reduce the costs to settle the estate?
- Do you want to reduce the taxes?
- Should you provide for your protection in the event of your incapacity?
- Do you have other objectives you want to accomplish?

Third, I recommend you see an attorney to help you plan your estate. (You certainly don't want to end up like the woman in California who left everything to the archbishop of San Diego when no archbishop of San Diego existed.) I'd recommend you see an attorney who specializes in estate planning.

Before you let your fingers do the walking, follow these pointers to find an attorney. First, after you've read this book, you'll know more about estate planning than most attorneys. (Remember reading about my friend, an attorney, who didn't realize you can act as trustee of your own trust?) We live in a day of specialization. For example, a medical doctor could be a brain surgeon or a podiatrist. It's the same way in the legal profession. We have divorce attorneys, bankruptcy attorneys, personal injury attorneys, corporate lawyers, criminal lawyers, and estate planning attorneys.

Keep in mind that any attorney will prepare a will for you. If you call one and say, "I'd like to have a will drawn," that's what you'll get. In fact, I was discussing this situation with a new client. He commented that he'd asked his attorney to draw up a will. My client divulged, "You know, that attorney was really nice. He spent an hour with me and my wife going over what we wanted in our will. Then he drafted this fine legal document. He called us back in and reviewed it with us. After we signed it, he gave it to us and charged us only $300 for all that work and time. I know he spent at least three hours on this project and he regularly charges $200 an hour. I thought he was a generous guy.

"Then, as my wife and I were leaving his office, he nonchalantly asked, 'By the way, what are you going to do with that will? Where will you keep it?' I responded that I didn't know. And he suggested, 'Let me keep it here in our fireproof vault for you.' After I left his office I realized the significance of leaving our will in the attorney's vault. Ha! When it was time to probate the will, the family would have to return to that lawyer to get the original will. Naturally, that clever lawyer would conduct the probate and, at that point, would make a considerable amount of money."

No matter what their specialty is, any attorney will draw a will for you. Some believe it's a public service and some, of course, want to handle the probate of the estate.

After you've read this book, I sincerely hope you're interested in more than having a will. Find an estate planning attorney to help with estate planning. Before you hire an attorney, you need to call a few and ask questions. Start with the list of "Twelve Costly Misconceptions" from Chapter Five. For example, ask point-blank if you can be your own trustee. If the attorney says, "No, you must have a bank involved," then find another attorney.

You're interested in a revocable living trust so ask a lot of questions about trusts. Ask if the attorney has drafted any revocable living trusts. Don't ask, "Do you know how to do it?" Many attorneys will say yes and then they'll learn on your case—and at your expense.

Don't forget (or don't be afraid) to ask how much it will cost to draft the trust. Be prepared for many different answers. Most attorneys are reluctant to quote a fee over the telephone and with valid reason. Some people just want to shop by phone, determined to find the cheapest price. They don't care about the services the attorneys provide or their specific experiences in particular areas. Some attorneys won't quote a figure until they know what kind of service you expect, what your needs are, and the complexity of the situation. But, usually, you can ask for and receive a ballpark figure.

Please don't think I disapprove of shopping around. Another client's story shows how important it is to be selective. This client, Mr. Shopper, is an officer for a large corporation. He came to see me after hearing me speak about trusts on a radio talk show. He explained that after the radio show, he visited the estate planning attorney in the law firm his corporation used. They visited awhile before the lawyer said, "Yes, you should have a revocable living trust and we can prepare one for you right here in this office for only $10,000." Well, Mr. Shopper got up off the floor and decided he'd better investigate further.

He spoke to his neighbor, who is an attorney, and asked, "What do you think about a revocable living trust?"

The attorney quickly replied, "Oh, no, you don't want to get involved in a revocable living trust. They're much too complicated. You need to have a bank involved as a trustee. Just put everything in joint tenancy, then come in and see me. We'll draw up a new will for you. That's all you need to do."

Because he had been somewhat educated by the talk show, Mr. Shopper wasn't satisfied with his neighbor's advice. Next, Mr. Shopper made an appointment to meet with me. After we visited awhile, we determined that he needed a revocable living trust to avoid probate. He had no tax problems so it was uncomplicated. It was a simple matter of setting up a trust to leave his property to his family without going through the probate court system. I prepared his trust for about $2,000—the same kind of trust he would have received for $10,000 at that first law firm. As you see, shopping around is important.

When attorneys quote their fees, be sure to find out what the fees include. Each attorney charges differently. After attending one of my seminars, Mrs. Transfer visited her accountant to prepare her taxes. When she asked him about a revocable living trust, he replied, "Yes, you should have one and here's a list of trust attorneys from which to choose."

So Mrs. Transfer made an appointment with one of those attorneys and he drew up a revocable living trust. It took him "only" five and a half months to do it! When she met with him to sign the trust, he gave her a bill for $2,250.

The attorney said, "Now that you have a revocable living trust, you need to transfer your assets into the trust. We need to prepare your transfer documents. A trust isn't any good on its own—it's empty. You have to re-title your property in the name of the trust. That means you have to file a deed for your home. I'll charge you $500 to do that. And then it will cost another $200 to transfer the stocks and the bonds." He continued to enumerate other items and additional costs. At that point, Mrs. Transfer stopped him and left his office.

Then she came to see me. After listening to her story, I shook my head and replied, "Oh, I wish you would have come to see me first. Your trust is fairly simple. We could have done all that for less than $2,500. And my fee would have included the deeds for transferring your property, the letters to the banks, and all the other transfer notices."

I explained that I could prepare the transfers to her trust but would have to charge her. She asked me to draw up the transfer papers.

Always ask attorneys what their fees include. An important question Mrs. Transfer should have asked was this: Does the fee include the transfer of property into the trust—the funding of the trust—after it is established? (*Funding* simply means that the attorney has re-titled all the assets to the name of your trust.)

Unfortunately, Mrs. Transfer wasn't my only client who experienced an encounter with an unknowledgeable attorney (or possibly a knowledgeable attorney who didn't care to explain all the consequences). Two of my clients, Mr. and Mrs. Everett, are a married couple who own a prospering construction company. They have five children and own several pieces of real estate. Early in their marriage, they had recognized the need for estate planning, so they had visited a large, "downtown" law firm and hired that firm's estate planning lawyer to prepare a trust for them. Their estate was large enough to be subject to an estate tax in the event of a death. For that reason, in conference with their attorney, they decided to have a trust with a provision for an A/B trust (a marital deduction) to save estate taxes. They paid the attorney nearly $10,000 for this estate plan.

Years later, the couple hired me to review their trust to ensure it was up to date and make any necessary revisions. I examined it and determined it was well drafted. Then I asked to review the pour-over will and the deeds transferring their six parcels of real estate into the trust. They told me no such deeds existed; their attorney hadn't made the transfers and hadn't told them this was necessary. But they were able to present a pour-over will. A quick assessment of the pour-over will revealed that there was no schedule of trust assets—the document that would list all their assets. Not one of their assets was titled in the name of their trust! Unbelievably, the trust was completely empty.

Even more unbelievably, their previous attorney had appointed himself as their personal representative! Since no deeds to the trust existed, the entire estate would require a probate because none of their assets were protected by the trust. What's more, because their A/B (marital deduction) trust was empty, the estate would need to go to probate twice—once upon the death of the first spouse and again upon the death of the second spouse!

Since the attorney had appointed himself as their personal representative, he would take the estate to probate—both times! The attorney could be paid as the personal representative as well as the attorney of the personal representative. And it was all legal.

The Everetts were furious. When they had created the trust, they hadn't understood the details or the ramifications of the attorney's costly paperwork. They threatened to sue the lawyer who had created their original trust. (Needless to say, that attorney is no longer their personal representative.) After they calmed down, I prepared a new trust for them. Obviously, this new trust included a new pour-over will. I also prepared six deeds to transfer their real estate into their new trust. In addition, I created an up-to-date schedule of trust assets and wrote letters to their banks and investment advisors with instructions to title the existing accounts into the trust name. Because the Everetts remained as the signers on all these documents, they kept complete control of all their investments. We determined that the Everetts also needed living wills with health-care directives and powers of attorney. I provided all this to their satisfaction at a cost much less than $10,000. Do you see how important it is to ask lawyers to explain exactly what their fees cover?

In another example, Mr. and Mrs. Olson had visited with me and nearly retained my services about six years ago. They had wanted to prepare a living trust but had decided to use an attorney who quoted a lesser fee than I had.

They came back to see me this year and showed me their estate documents. They had, indeed, hired another attorney to prepare their living trust. However, the paperwork was full of legalese and they never did understand it. When their family situation changed, they decided to come back to see me. I agreed to prepare a new trust for them—one they could understand.

As I studied their first trust, I discovered that it had never been funded! None of their assets had been re-titled into the name of that trust. I performed all the transfers of their real estate, stocks, bonds, bank accounts, and other investments. I made sure the trust was named as the contingent beneficiary on all of their IRAs and prepared a new pour-over will. I also suggested they create health-care powers of attorney, prepare living wills, and sign a general durable power of attorney.

I explained that their estate would have been subject to probate because the titles to all their assets had been in their personal names. Probate would have cost their estate ten times as much as the fee I had quoted them in the first consultation.

Once everything was signed, Mr. and Mrs. Olson relaxed. They commented, "We wish we had done it right the first time. It would have been less costly and we would have had peace of mind." Sometimes the lower fee can be the more expensive option in the long run. Don't choose the less expensive option to "save" money.

Questions to Ask an Estate Planning Attorney

- Is the attorney experienced with revocable living trusts?
- What kind of service can I expect? Can I call and ask questions if problems arise?
- Does your office charge for phone calls?
- Will I counsel directly with an attorney or will I be talking with the office paralegal?

After a woman had attended one of my presentations on revocable living trusts, she sent her mother in San Jose some of my information on revocable living trusts and wills. Her mother, Mrs. Small, liked what she read and believed she should have a revocable living trust.

When she called her attorney to discuss the matter, he replied, "I don't do any revocable living trusts, but I'll give you the names of some trust lawyers." The first attorney Mrs. Small called quipped, "I'm really too busy to get involved in that right now. Your $250,000 estate is too small for a trust. I don't want to handle it."

The next attorney declared, "I'll set up a trust for you but to quote you my fee, I'll need to see a list of your assets, showing their total appraised value. Not just an estimate; I need a bona fide appraisal."

Frustrated, Mrs. Small called me and pleaded, "I'm coming to see my daughter for Thanksgiving. If I send you the information ahead of time, can we set up a trust and sign it while I'm in Phoenix?" I was happy to accommodate. The week she visited, we signed her trust and set up her estate plan—without appraising one single item!

Action Items—Chapter 7: It's Time to "Just Do It!"

Take a moment to complete the following action items.

Action 1: Review the 14 Tough Questions to Ask an Attorney Before You Write a Check

Action 2: Find an attorney who specializes in estate planning—Contact attorneys who specialize in estate planning to find out if they draft revocable living trusts (or you can call me). Follow the advice in this chapter to ask questions to determine which attorney will best meet your needs. Here are the key questions to ask:

- Have you drafted revocable living trusts? If yes, how many?
- How much does the whole process cost? How do you determine your fees?
- What do your fees include? Please give me specifics.

Go to *www.EstatePlanningDr.com/book* to download:

14 Tough Questions to Ask An Attorney Before You Write a Check

Chapter Eight

Keeping Your Assets Safe from Lawsuits, Creditors, and Judgments

How will you transfer wealth to your children and grandchildren? How can you protect your assets from lawsuits and creditors? Beyond revocable living trusts, a number of trusts and other solutions are available to your family, including the family limited partnership, irrevocable life insurance trust, charitable remainder trust, personal residence trust, asset protection trust, and liquid asset protection plan.

Family Limited Partnership (FLP)

In the early 1900s, people set up partnerships for business purposes. This was, and still is, one of the worst ways to own business assets. It indicates all partners are jointly and severally liable, meaning that each partner is totally at risk for the debts and liabilities of every other partner. With the introduction of a limited partnership, each partner's liability is limited to only the amount that each individual partner contributed to the partnership. This legal process produces two positive results: the partners are protected and it encourages people to do business.

The limited partnership concept has caught on with business owners as well as business and estate planners. It's touted as one of the best methods to protect assets from creditors, predators, and lawsuits. You may also use a limited partnership to transfer wealth from one generation to another while reducing the costs of the transfers and still maintaining control over assets.

A family limited partnership is becoming one of the most popular methods to protect your assets. A family limited partnership (FLP) allows you to begin shifting ownership of your estate to your heirs and achieve certain tax benefits without losing control of your estate—all while protecting the assets from creditors and lawsuits.

Here's how an FLP works: You write a limited partnership agreement that defines two distinct classes of partners—general partner and limited partner. The general partner has complete control, management, and decision-making authority over all business of the partnership. The limited partner is the owner of the equity or value of the partnership assets but doesn't have voting or management rights. You transfer certain assets (those which you desire to protect from judgments and liabilities) into the name of the partnership. You make this transfer in exchange for limited partnership interests represented by something similar to stock certificates, called units. This action creates the partnership.

The partnership agreement names the general, or managing, partner. The person creating the partnership (or that person's limited liability company) is usually the initial controlling general partner and is also the original limited partner because of the exchange of assets for units. You begin your family limited partnership as both the general and limited partner in most cases. Then your attorney files a certificate of limited partnership with the appropriate state authority.

As I noted above, the family limited partnership is one of the best methods to protect your assets from lawsuits and creditors. You may also use the FLP to transfer wealth from one generation to another. The FLP allows you to make a gift of limited partnership interests (units) to your children or heirs in order to reduce the size of your estate without placing cash or property directly in the control of your heirs. For example, you make a gift of some of your limited partnership interests to your family members or others of your choice. As general partner, you retain control over the use and nature of the assets in your family limited partnership.

The partnership owns whatever you place into it. As an example, let's say you own a vacation home valued at $200,000 and place it into your family limited

Transferor

Family Limited Partnership

Family Members Limited Partners

General Partner

Family Limited Partnership

partnership. Now the partnership owns the vacation home instead of you individually. If you wish to give your children an ownership interest in your vacation home, you're actually giving them an ownership interest in the partnership. Your children may use the home for their own vacations. However, your children have no control over your vacation home or the partnership.

A major advantage of an FLP is the benefit of non-taxable gifting. Each year you may give a gift of up to $12,000 (the annual federal gift tax exclusion limit) to any individual or individuals you choose. The government doesn't impose taxes on this gift to either you or the people who receive your gift. FLP interests (units) are easily divided, thus enabling you to take full advantage of the annual exclusion limits. An FLP allows you (the general partner) to gift your children a portion of the value of your vacation house by giving a chosen number of partnership units. In other words, you're actually giving your children units of ownership, not cash or actual title to real property.

Plus you're giving only a portion of your partnership units (let's say 5 percent of the units), but no power or control over the partnership. So the IRS, for good reason, considers that portion less valuable than the equivalent percentage (5 percent) of the value of the vacation house, which in this example is $10,000. The deemed, or considered, value or your gift may be only $7,500. This enables your heirs to receive a partnership share at a discounted rate.

Mrs. Smart and Her Daughter

Mrs. Smart owns a house worth $100,000. This year, using an FLP, Mrs. Smart decides to gift her daughter 20 percent of the value of her house that is in her family limited partnership. This appears to be simple math: Mrs. Smart's gift is worth $20,000, which exceeds the annual exclusion for gift taxes. At first Mrs. Smart thinks she herself may be taxed on this gift. But no! Because Mrs. Smart is gifting only a portion of her house by way of a partnership interest—and her daughter doesn't own the total asset—the value of the gift for tax purposes isn't worth as much as the proportionate share of the house that Mrs. Smart gifted to her daughter. In other words, she actually made a gift of 20 percent of the interest in the partnership (an actual equity value of $20,000), yet the discounted value of her gift is less than $12,000. This is because restrictions exist in how partnership units are transferred; they can't easily be sold on the open market.

In this way, Mrs. Smart passes the assets in her family limited partnership from her estate to her daughter at a discounted rate. Meanwhile, Mrs. Smart retains control of her estate and protects her assets from lawsuits.

Here are three additional reasons why the family limited partnership is becoming a popular staple of estate planning.

Reason 1: FLPs must file income tax returns—The yearly return shows the proportion of equity each limited partner owns. The FLP enables a parent or grandparent to divert income from the partnership assets to their children and grandchildren. Generally, those children and grandchildren are in lower tax brackets so the heirs pay fewer taxes on the partnership income than the general partner would have had to pay.

Reason 2: Upon the death of a limited partner, his respective rights in the FLP become an asset of his estate but at a discounted value for tax purposes—Upon the death of the limited partner, the respective units of ownership of the FLP (think of them as stock certificates) are transferred to the heirs according to the terms of that partner's revocable living trust. Yes, it's still necessary to have a trust even with a family limited partnership to avoid probate and, thus, to avoid a disruption in the ownership of the partnership equity (represented by the partnership units).

According to the written partnership agreement, the partnership units have some restrictions on their transferability. For this and other reasons, the value of the partnership units is somewhat less than the actual value of the assets held in the partnership. This is called a *discounted value*. That means there will be less value in the decedent's estate to determine if any estate tax is due.

In addition, the decedent may have been the managing member of the LLC, which serves as the general partner of the FLP. The decedent's revocable living trust will address the change in the managing member. Therefore, the business of the FLP won't be disrupted.

Reason 3: To a certain degree, an FLP provides protection against lawsuits—Certain characteristics of the way in which the partnership ownership is organized make it attractive as a means to safeguard your assets.

How FLPs Protect Your Assets

To explain an FLP further, partners hold the family limited partnership property in a special form. Each person's rights in the partnership are spelled out in the partnership agreement. Partnership assets aren't subject to the debts of either the general partner (the person who owns the estate) or the limited partners (the heirs to the estate). An FLP won't require you to become a partner with anyone with whom you don't choose to partner (such as a prodigal child or a creditor). For this reason, the law has created a method for relief against a partnership.

In other words, you may ask, "What remedy is available to a creditor for a claim against the partnership?" It's this: The court allows a judgment creditor to obtain relief through a "charging order," which allows the creditor to receive the income that would be allocated to that judgment debtor by reason of the judgment debtor's ownership of such partner's partnership interest. For instance, if a creditor is awarded a judgment against one of the partners, the creditor can apply for a charging order—a court order to enforce the judgment that will affect only the partnership interest of the partner who owes the debt. Therefore, if the partnership pays any income to the debtor partner, the partnership must now pay that amount to the creditor who holds the judgment. The creditor doesn't become a partner of the FLP but is entitled to receive any income distributions that would otherwise be payable to the debtor partner.

Creditors who obtain a charging order against a family limited partnership (FLP) should be aware of the following facts. The general partner of an FLP can choose to either distribute the partnership income or accumulate this income and reinvest it in the FLP. The partnership doesn't pay taxes on that income; the individual partners pay the taxes. Whether the general partner decides to distribute the income from the FLP or not, he must issue a K-1 tax report to all the limited partners. (A K-1 tax report is part of the partnership tax return showing each partner's share of the partnership income.) Even if the general partner decides to reinvest the income instead of making a distribution, he must issue a K-1 tax report showing each partner's share and tax liability. In that situation, the creditors receive the K-1 tax report that would have been sent to the judgment debtor. However, the creditors will receive no money because no distribution has been made from the partnership. Therefore the judgment creditor will have to pay taxes on income that was never actually distributed. This is often referred to as *phantom income*. This is why most attorneys recommend their clients don't try to collect a judgment against someone with an interest in an FLP. Do you see how the FLP offers valuable protection for assets inside it?

In another example, Mr. Tannenbaum, an astute and successful businessman, has a large family. He wants to teach his adult children stewardship so he places much of his wealth in a family limited partnership. He controls the partnership through one of his limited liability companies, which was named as the general partner. His revocable living trust is the major limited partner. He advised all his children to establish their own revocable living trusts. Every year, Mr. Tannenbaum gifts limited partnership interests to each of his children as their sole and separate property, to be held in their respective trusts. He gradually reduces the size of his estate by making these gifts at discounted values. He asks the children, as limited partners, to be involved in making some of the decisions affecting the assets held by this family partnership. In this manner, he can involve them in the businesses or investments and teach them stewardship. Each year when his accountant prepares the tax return for the partnership, it shows that the children were responsible for the income on the partnership share represented by their limited partnership interest, even though they had no real control of the assets.

The father, in his benevolent manner, plowed all of the income earned by the partnership back into the partnership. He advises his children to prepare their individual income tax returns two ways: one showing their income without the partnership share and one including their distributive share as limited partners of the FLP.

Why prepare two tax returns? The partnership itself pays no tax; however, the individual partners pay tax on their percentage of ownership. The children are thrilled to learn that even though their father (the general managing partner) reinvested most of the partnership income in the partnership, he would distribute enough income to them to pay the increase in taxes caused by having to report their share of the partnership income on their tax returns.

Some of the children were also happy to learn that if anyone took them to court and they experienced an adverse outcome, the creditor who won the judgment would have no right against the partnership property. The creditor could only obtain a charging order. That means the interest of a limited partner against whom a judgment had been entered would be charged with the requirement to pay the judgment out of partnership distributions. During those years, the general partner may decide not to make any distributions from the partnership. Any judgment creditors who would have charging orders against a limited partner's interest would then receive the K-1, or tax report, of the partner's share of the distributed income. Even if no income is actually distributed, judgment creditors would have to report this income as received on their own tax returns. They would be required to pay the tax on this share, even though they receive nothing—a "phantom income."

By using a family limited partnership, Mr. Tannenbaum reduces the size of his taxable estate by making gifts of partnership interests each year to his children. Because of the discounted values, the FLP enables him to reduce his estate more quickly than by any other method. The children are learning stewardship over business assets. The children paid taxes on their share of the partnership income, which is taxed at a lower rate because the income is attributed to the children, who are in a lower tax bracket than their wealthy father. Plus the partnership assets are protected from lawsuits and judgments against the father or any of the children.

The family limited partnership creates a wonderful, win-win situation for the Tannenbaum family.

Advantages of Using a Family Limited Partnership

- Asset protection
- Opportunity for the general partner to make larger, tax-free gifts than would otherwise be possible
- May reduce estate tax without giving up any control over assets
- Opportunity for the general partner to achieve a lower tax rate by dividing FLP income among limited partners, and creditors, if any
- Opportunity for parents and grandparents to teach children and grandchildren stewardship over business assets without giving up control

---

> ### Disadvantages of Using a Family Limited Partnership
>
> - You must file an income tax return for the partnership.
> - The FLP must have a business purpose. (However, this is easily accomplished. For example, you can simply define "managing the property" or something similar as the business purpose of an FLP.)
> - Establishing a family limited partnership is costly (the average cost is approximately $3,000 to $4,000).

Irrevocable Life Insurance Trust (ILIT)

To keep their assets safe from lawsuits, creditors, and judgments, some people choose the irrevocable life insurance trust. First, let's dispel the most common misconception about life insurance: that the death benefits are received tax free. It's true that death benefits are free of income tax. However, they may be subject to estate tax. If you're named as the owner of your life-insurance policy, or have the right to change the beneficiaries, or personally pay the insurance premiums, the benefit payable upon your death will be included in your estate and an estate tax may be due. By having these rights while you're alive (called *incidents of ownership*), this makes your insurance proceeds part of your taxable estate.

No one wants to pay tax on life-insurance proceeds. Rest assured, your life insurance is one of the easiest assets to remove from your taxable estate.

The irrevocable life insurance trust (ILIT) is an irrevocable trust that holds assets outside of your estate. You no longer have an incident of ownership in the life insurance; the irrevocable trust will exempt these assets from estate taxes upon your death. You and your attorney can name an ILIT as the owner and beneficiary of your life insurance policy. This will ensure that the insurance proceeds are passed to the beneficiaries without first being taxed. To avoid the tax on the insurance, your ILIT must be irrevocable and you must appoint someone other than yourself to be its trustee.

The benefits of the irrevocable life insurance trust are many:

Fewer taxes—Because the ILIT now owns the insurance policy, you retain no ownership interest. The proceeds of your insurance won't be included in your taxable estate upon your death. The life insurance policy will pay death benefits to your heirs according to your instructions in your ILIT, without tax and without probate.

Gift-tax exclusion—To satisfy gift-tax requirements, the beneficiaries of your ILIT have specific withdrawal powers. This provision allows you, the grantor, to make tax-free gift contributions to the ILIT to pay premiums on the insurance that the ILIT holds.

Liquid funds to pay taxes—Upon your death, your estate will need to pay its debts, costs, and taxes. If your estate isn't liquid, the trustee of your irrevocable life insurance trust may allow the ILIT to make loans to your estate or allow the ILIT to purchase assets from your estate. Such loans or payments from the irrevocable life insurance trust aren't included in your taxable estate and allows liquidity.

How do you determine if you need an irrevocable life insurance trust?

Add up your taxable estate—When you die, the government considers everything that's in your name and that you control to be in your taxable estate. Remember, your taxable estate includes your life insurance death benefit if you're the owner, if you retain the right to change the beneficiaries, or if you pay the premiums directly.

Determine your applicable exclusion amount—Refer to Figure 4.1 in Chapter Four to find out your applicable exclusion amount.

Calculate the amount on which you will pay estate taxes—Federal taxes are due on all assets valued over the applicable exclusion amount. In the case of a married couple with a tax-saving A/B trust (or marital deduction trust), taxes are due only on assets valued at more than twice the applicable exclusion amount. For example, the applicable exclusion amount in 2007 is $2 million. If you and your spouse have a revocable living trust with an A/B trust provision and the value of your estate in 2007 is approximately $5 million, the estate must pay taxes on $1 million should you both die in that year. *Note that estate tax currently ranges from 37 to 50 percent.*

If your life insurance death benefit puts you in the position of owing estate taxes, you should create an ILIT or use a family limited partnership to remove that asset from your taxable estate.

Establishing an irrevocable life insurance trust to assume ownership of your life insurance policies will remove those policies from your taxable estate. Since the trust is irrevocable and because you aren't the trustee, the IRS no longer considers the insurance proceeds part of your taxable estate.

IRREVOCABLE INSURANCE TRUST

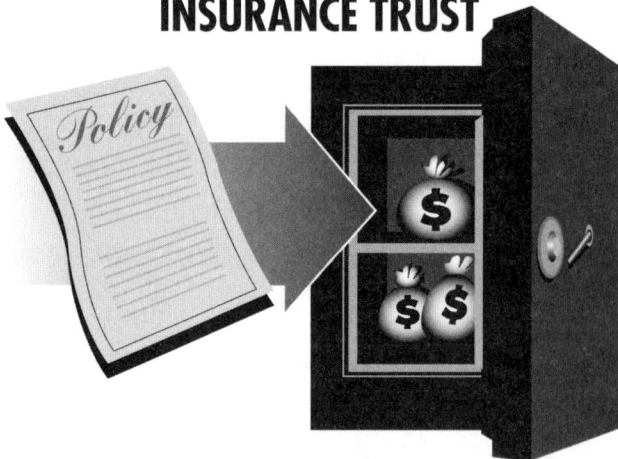

• Pays Estate Taxes
• Provides Liquidity

Answers to Common Questions about ILITs

Still unsure about ILITs and whether they can benefit you and your family? Read on to learn the answers to the most common questions regarding irrevocable life insurance trusts.

In a nutshell, what is an ILIT?—An irrevocable life insurance trust is a type of living trust that can't be altered, amended, or revoked by the grantor—the person who sets up the trust. This type of trust owns life insurance policies, authorizes the trustee (someone other than the grantor) to pay premiums from the ILIT funds when due, and designates the distribution of life insurance proceeds to the ILIT beneficiaries.

The ILIT has the following characteristics:

- You retain no interest or power. Thus, upon your death, the proceeds of your insurance aren't included in your taxable estate.
- The beneficiaries enjoy withdrawal powers that allow you, the grantor, to make contributions to the ILIT—to pay premiums on the insurance held by the ILIT and to use the gift-tax exclusion.
- The trustee has the power to purchase assets from or make loans to your estate to pay any debts, costs, or taxes to settle your estate. These payments are excluded from your taxable estate while providing estate liquidity.

Why should an insurance trust be irrevocable?—If you retain the right to revoke the trust or if you act as the trustee, the assets owned by the trust will still be included in your estate for tax purposes. To avoid the tax on the insurance, your trust must be irrevocable and you must appoint someone other than yourself to be the trustee.

Why do I need an irrevocable life insurance trust?—If your estate is above the applicable exclusion amount, placing life insurance policies in an ILIT will reduce your taxable estate by the amount of the life insurance death benefit. With this type of trust, your life insurance proceeds won't be subject to any federal estate taxes whatsoever.

When you die, everything in your name and what you control are considered to be in your taxable estate. If you don't have an ILIT, your taxable estate also includes the amount of death benefits paid by your life insurance. Remember, your estate must pay federal estate taxes on all assets valued at more than the applicable exclusion amount shown in Figure 4.1 in Chapter Four.

You may establish an irrevocable life insurance trust that will assume ownership of existing insurance policies or purchase new policies. The ILIT authorizes the trustee to pay the insurance premiums from funds you have contributed as gifts, tax-free to the ILIT. The ILIT will also be the beneficiary of your life insurance. Because the trust is irrevocable and you aren't the trustee, the insurance proceeds aren't considered part of your taxable estate when you die.

What problems have people encountered with ILITs?—Irrevocable life insurance trusts can encounter the following types of problems:

1. Pre-existing policies transferred to the trust will be brought back into the taxable estate if the grantor—the person who sets up the trust—dies within three years of the transfer.
2. This type of trust is irrevocable. Once you establish your insurance trust, you can't alter or amend it. Your insurance policies are owned by your trust.
3. Contributions to the trust may cause a gift tax.

Can you set up the ILIT to overcome the problems listed above?—Yes, you can set up the ILIT to overcome these problems in the following ways:

1. To overcome the first problem of pre-existing policies, thanks to modern life-insurance actuarial schedules and administration techniques, sometimes it's easier and more cost effective to replace an existing insurance policy with a new policy owned by the ILIT. Assuming you're still insurable, replacing existing insurance allows the ILIT to be the original owner of the insurance and the three-year rule won't apply. Thus, the insurance won't be included in your estate for tax purposes. But you need to consider the costs and advantages of replacing such

policies. If it isn't possible to replace them, the three-year rule will apply. However, when you consider the estate tax savings, betting that you'll live for the three years is worth gambling the cost of setting up the ILIT.

2. To overcome the second problem—irrevocability— the ILIT contains an escape hatch that can help you avoid this problem. The trust assets can be restored to the grantor (you) through a special power of appointment clause. This special power would permit the grantor's spouse to appoint the assets back to the grantor without adverse tax consequences. The person holding this power can't exercise it for his own benefit. The major problem with this provision is that the grantor may not always be able to control the spouse's decision.

3. To overcome the third problem—contributions may cause a gift tax—the ILIT eliminates the gift-tax problem by incorporating "crummey" withdrawal rights for the ILIT beneficiaries. (You'll learn more about "crummey" below.) This allows you to make a gift to the ILIT of up to $12,000 annually for each ILIT beneficiary without incurring any gift tax. For example, if you have five beneficiaries and you give each of them $12,000 every year, you can give $60,000 annually as gift-tax free.

What are "crummey" withdrawal rights?—After a gift has been made to the irrevocable life insurance trust, the ILIT trustee must notify the ILIT beneficiaries that a gift has been made, usually by sending a Notice of Contribution, also known as *crummey letter*. The beneficiaries have the right to ask that the value of their shares be given to them. These withdrawal rights are temporary and usually last only 30 to 45 days.

Why is this called a *crummey letter*? This technique was established in the court case of Crummey versus Commissioner in 1968. Named after Mr. Crummey, these rights have become known as *Crummey Powers*. Mr. Crummey was a taxpayer who was sued by the IRS for claiming that gifts made to his irrevocable trust to pay insurance premiums were completed gifts. This made the insurance held in his irrevocable trust become an asset outside of his estate for estate tax purposes. The Commissioner was the head of the Internal Revenue Service. He disagreed with Mr. Crummey and wanted the death benefit to be included as a part of the taxable estate. Mr. Crummey won the case.

The ILIT trustee must tell the ILIT beneficiaries that these rights to withdraw the amount of the gift made to the trust exist in the trust beneficiaries. In other words, the beneficiaries may take the amount of any gifts to the trust as their own money. However, if they do this, there wouldn't be any money left to pay the insurance policy premiums.

Crummey withdrawal rights aren't designed to be exercised. Instead, they're designed only to qualify the ILIT for the annual gift-tax exclusion. Most beneficiaries won't exercise their Crummey powers and withdraw money from the ILIT. This might make it difficult to pay the premium due on the policy because the withdrawal could deplete the funds that were contributed by you, the grantor, for the purpose of paying the premium. In short, if the policy's premium isn't paid, the policy could become defunct and the beneficiary won't receive any death benefits.

Do I need to set up my ILIT more than three years before my death to ensure the value of my insurance isn't included in my taxable estate?—The ILIT insulates any policy it holds from federal estate tax if you transferred the policy to your ILIT more than three years preceding your death. If you should die within three years of the time the ILIT acquires the policy, the IRS would argue that the insurance should be included in your taxable estate. To avoid this possibility, consider having the ILIT apply for and purchase a new policy.

Whom should I choose as trustee of my ILIT?—You may not act as the trustee of an ILIT that holds insurance on your life; doing so would cause the insurance proceeds to be included in your taxable estate. Choices for trustee include other trusted family members (as long as they aren't minors, your spouse, or members of your household), friends, relatives, professionals (such as an attorney or accountant), and corporations in the business of delivering trust services. You should have a great deal of faith and confidence in the person you appoint and be able to work well with that person, bank, or company.

The main drawbacks of appointing a corporate trustee (a bank or company) are the annual administration fees and the occasional inability of the corporate trustee to relate to the needs of the ILIT beneficiaries. Some people create a trust and appoint a professional or a family member as the trustee—and charge that person with transferring the assets for investment purposes to a corporate trustee once the grantor has died and policy proceeds are paid. This helps the trust avoid paying unnecessary annual administration fees until a substantial trust estate exists.

The main drawback of having a family member or other individual act as the trustee of your ILIT is that the individual may not be as disciplined or as reliable as a bank or trust company. For example, the trustee must ensure a procedure exists to receive the gift to pay the premiums on the insurance policy. The trustee must then notify the trust beneficiaries that they have the right to withdraw their share of the gift for the next 30 (or so) days and remind them that they shouldn't make a withdrawal. (If beneficiaries make withdrawals, the insurance premiums might not be paid, the insurance policy could lapse, and the death benefit wouldn't be paid, which would result in reducing the beneficiaries' overall inheritance.) Assuming the funds aren't withdrawn, the trustee must remember to pay the insurance premium. These responsibilities require reminders, procedures, diplomacy, and discipline.

Why should the ILIT be the beneficiary of my insurance policy?—If you name your ILIT as beneficiary, the insurance company will pay the proceeds to the ILIT and your trustee can then use the funds according to the instructions you put in your ILIT. For example, your ILIT's trustee could purchase assets from your revocable living trust, replacing hard assets with cash to pay income and estate taxes to prevent a distress sale of your assets.

Also, if one of your beneficiaries is incompetent or incapacitated when you die, your trustee can invest that beneficiary's share and provide for his care for as long as needed. If you had named that person as a beneficiary of the life insurance policy, the insurance company probably wouldn't pay your beneficiary directly but would insist on court supervision through a conservatorship. Therefore, your ILIT should be both the owner *and* the beneficiary of the insurance policy.

How are the insurance premiums paid when I have an ILIT?—Once a year (or as often as needed), the grantor (you) contributes enough cash to the ILIT to pay any upcoming insurance premiums. After the grantor makes this gift to the ILIT—and after the time the trust agreement allows for the trust beneficiaries to withdraw this gift—the trustee writes a check from the ILIT's bank account to pay the premiums to the insurance company. (Because a tax-payer identification number is required for a bank account, you must file an application for an employer identification number, Form SS-4, with the IRS.) The grantor (or insured) should *never* pay premiums directly to the insurance company.

Community Property States

If you live in a community property state and want to transfer existing insurance policies to an irrevocable life insurance trust, take note. Nine states are considered community-property states: Arizona, California, Idaho, Louisiana, Nevada, New Mexico, Texas, Washington, and Wisconsin. These states have community property laws, which means that all property that either spouse acquires during the marriage is considered to be owned by both spouses. This property isn't considered to be separate property unless it's acquired as a gift, as an inheritance, or is disclaimed by the other spouse. All earnings from the personal efforts of either spouse are considered earnings by both spouses and, therefore, belong to both spouses. All income derived from this community property is also considered to be owned by both spouses.

In these states, the ILIT won't totally accomplish its intended purpose if any of the existing insurance policies can be classified as community property. The IRS will determine a life insurance policy is community property if:

- It's acquired by a married couple while the couple resides in a community property state.
- The couple uses community funds to pay premiums.
- The couple doesn't take affirmative action to show that one spouse gave his or her community interest to the other, which would convert the property to that spouse's sole and separate property.

If the grantor's spouse dies before the grantor and the policy is classified as community property, then the estate of the grantor's spouse must include one-half of the value of the community interest in the taxable estate.

The disposition of property at death is governed by the laws of the state in which the person lived at the time of death. However, insurance policy proceeds are attributed to the decedent's estate according to the property rights already established in that policy—either as community property or as sole and separate property.

An irrevocable life insurance trust can become complicated in states with community property laws. The key to avoiding these complications is to make sure the life insurance policies are characterized as the sole and separate property of the grantor to the ILIT. When you transfer an existing policy to the trust, the grantor's spouse should take affirmative action to convert each policy into the sole and separate property of the grantor. Thus, the grantor who owns the policy as sole and separate property may transfer it directly to the irrevocable life insurance trust without any community property strings attached.

How does the grantor's spouse take "affirmative action" to show the policy is the sole and separate property of the grantor? Complete a document titled Release of Community Property Interest to convert the community interest of an existing insurance policy to the sole and separate interest of the grantor to transfer the policy to the ILIT. Be sure to complete a separate release for each policy transferred to the ILIT. These releases are considered gifts, which avoids federal gift taxes thanks to the marital deduction. Take care to ensure the policy is identified on the insurance company's records as the grantor's sole and separate property.

By the way, if you're purchasing a new policy through your ILIT, then the release of community property interest isn't necessary.

Advantages and Disadvantages of an Irrevocable Life Insurance Trust

- Removes your life insurance from your taxable estate
- Provides liquid funds to settle your estate or to pay estate taxes
- Offers the least expensive, tax-free way for your heirs to pay off death taxes and settlement costs or to inherit a larger bequest

---

> ### Disadvantages of an Irrevocable
> ### Life Insurance Trust
>
> • Some advantages of ownership of your life insurance policies may be lost
> • Additional accounting and a tax return may be required
> • Grantor may be subject to the "gifts in contemplation of death" rules (the three-year rule)
> • Withdrawal (crummey) letters must be sent to the beneficiaries each time a contribution is made to the irrevocable life insurance trust

Charitable Remainder Trust

Charitable giving is a great way to reduce the size of a taxable estate. A charitable remainder trust (CRT) is one method of charitable giving. Using a CRT, you can actually give your assets away and keep them. It's like having your cake and eating it, too! Combined with an irrevocable life insurance trust (sometimes also called a *wealth replacement insurance trust*), a CRT allows you to pass your estate to your heirs tax free. You may even be able to increase the principal amount you can give to your heirs. Charitable giving has always been a fundamental aspect of estate planning. Many people have a strong sense of family and community and are inclined to make charitable gifts a part of their overall estate plan.

Choose an estate planning attorney who has a good understanding of charitable planning. This knowledge is extremely important given the complex nature of the charitable giving provisions of the Internal Revenue Code. While I encourage you to give to charities, don't approach the area of charitable planning lightly. Consider a myriad of issues such as control; income tax, gift tax, and estate tax ramifications; your current finances; your future income and principal needs; the extent of your charitable inclination; and the types of property you own.

Common Questions about Charitable Remainder Trusts

Charitable remainder trusts are complex. Here are a few of the most common questions people ask as they're determining if having a CRT is right for them.

In a nutshell, what is a charitable remainder trust?—This type of trust is an irrevocable trust created to hold assets given to the trust by a donor (you), either during your lifetime or upon your death.

A CRT is a type of split-interest trust. It shares its donated assets between noncharitable beneficiaries and charitable beneficiaries. Noncharitable beneficiaries are also called *income beneficiaries.* Typically, a CRT is designed to pay income to one or more *noncharitable beneficiaries* (usually the donor and the donor's spouse) either for life or for a term of years. Upon expiration of that time, the CRT assets are paid to or held for qualified charitable beneficiaries named in the trust agreement.

The CRT can't pay less than 5 percent of the value of the CRT assets to the income beneficiaries. CRT regulations don't limit the number or type of income beneficiaries; these can be individuals, corporations, trusts, and so on. However, at least one income beneficiary must be a taxable entity. Therefore, unborn individuals (such as grandchildren not yet born when you create the CRT) don't qualify as income beneficiaries unless the duration of the CRT is limited to a term of years.

A CRT can continue either for the lifetimes of the people selected as income beneficiaries or for a certain number of years (not to exceed 20 years). When the last income beneficiary dies or the term of years expires, all assets remaining in the CRT must be distributed to one or more charities, called *charitable remaindermen.* The charitable remaindermen are the charitable organizations that you have chosen to receive your ultimate charitable gift. This could be your favorite university, your church, or any approved charitable organization such as American Red Cross, Make-A-Wish Foundation, or United Way of America.

How does a CRT work?—To understand how a charitable remainder trust works, let's look at a typical CRT situation.

Mr. and Mrs. Smith have stock for which they paid $10,000. The stock has grown in value over the years and is now worth $110,000. It pays them a dividend of $1,500 a year, which is a return of 1.36 percent. Mr. and Mrs. Smith are both 61 years old. Their total estate is large enough for this stock to be taxable in their estate at a 50 percent marginal tax rate.

If the Smiths sell the stock, they'll have a capital gain of $100,000 ($110,000 sale price, less $10,000 basis). Their federal capital-gains tax rate is currently 15 percent. Accordingly, if the Smiths sell the stock, they will pay a $15,000 capital gains tax, leaving them with only $95,000 ($110,000 sales price, less $15,000 tax) to invest. If they invest the $95,000 and receive a 7 percent return, they'll receive only $6,650 in yearly income.

Instead of selling the stock, the Smiths can create a charitable remainder trust and donate their stock to it. The CRT then sells the stock. Since the CRT is charitable in nature, it pays no capital gains tax. Accordingly, the CRT now has $110,000 to invest.

The Smiths can write into the CRT that they want a 7 percent annual income for life from the CRT. They will then receive $7,700 a year in income. This income will continue to be paid to the Smiths—or, after one of them dies, to the surviving spouse—for life. Upon the death of both Mr. and Mrs. Smith, the balance of the funds in the CRT will be paid to the charity that Mr. and Mrs. Smith designated.

When the Smiths sign their charitable remainder trust and contribute their stock to it, they're making a charitable contribution of a portion of the value of the stock. The value of the charitable deduction that the Smiths receive is the value of the gift at the time of contribution, less the present value of the income projected to the Smiths on the basis of their actuarial life expectancies. In this case, they receive a charitable deduction of $23,770 (based on a 7 percent rate from IRS tables for the month of contribution), which will also save income tax.

Because the Smiths placed the stock into an irrevocable trust, the $110,000 is removed from the Smith's estate for estate-tax purposes, thus saving $55,000 in estate taxes ($110,000 x 50 percent marginal estate-tax rate).

It's common for a donor to a CRT to establish an irrevocable life insurance trust. The amount of insurance in the ILIT may be equal to or greater than the value of the asset you contribute to the CRT. This way, the insurance proceeds in the amount of the gift given to the charity may be distributed to the beneficiaries you name in your ILIT. The beneficiaries receive the death benefit distribution tax free.

For example, in the above scenario regarding the Smiths, they might create a wealth replacement insurance trust, or ILIT. They purchase a "second to die" life insurance policy by making a gift to the ILIT of a portion of the income they continue to receive from their CRT. The amount of insurance they purchase is equal to the amount of the gift they have made to the CRT. This insurance policy's death benefit will be paid upon the death of the second spouse. This means the death benefit will be at least $110,000, which is the amount necessary to replace their gift to the CRT. This amount will be paid by the trustee of the ILIT to the Smith's children at the time described in the ILIT. Because these funds come from the ILIT, they won't be included in the Smith's estate for estate tax purposes. Isn't that a little like having your cake and eating it too?

Can I actually "make money" by giving to charity?— If you plan your charitable gift wisely, the combination of tax savings and financial benefits can make your charitable sacrifice quite painless. In fact, you'll probably feel you've come out ahead, all things considered. In the previous example, the Smiths receive $7,700 a year income, which is $1,050 more a year than they received before creating their charitable remainder trust. In addition, they offset their income tax by the deduction for the charitable contribution. Upon their deaths, their heirs receive the insurance proceeds completely tax free. And the charity they selected receives whatever is left of the original gift. That means that the value of the gift the Smiths gave to their favorite charity is completely replaced by the death benefit from the insurance proceeds in their ILIT. Everyone comes out ahead, except for Uncle Sam. The key is careful—and proper—planning.

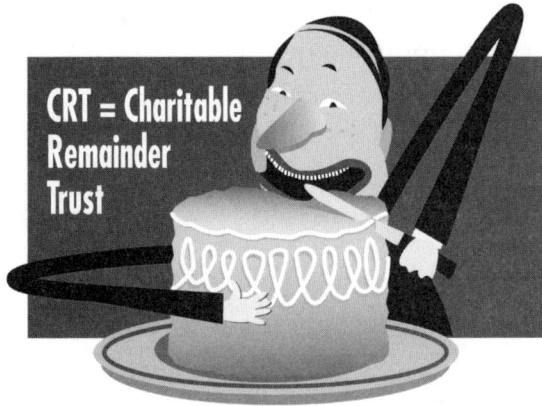

CRT = Charitable Remainder Trust

Have your cake and eat it too!

STEP #1

Transfer Assets into Charitable Remainder Trust

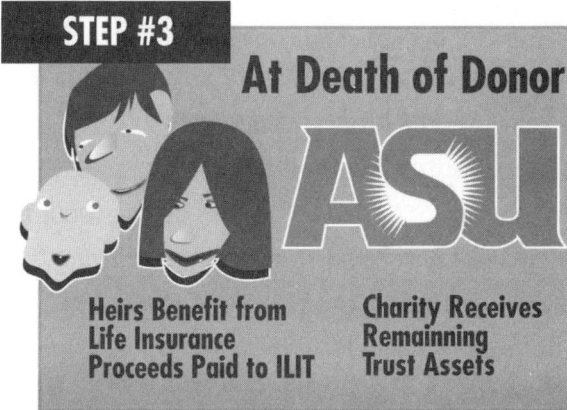

What is the simplest and most common way to make a gift?—Many people give to charity because they believe they can benefit society by giving to organizations they care about. If you have any charitable organization you want to help—for example, the church you attend, the school or college from which you or your children graduated, or the hospital that cared for loved ones—then, through a CRT, you can "profit," as well as derive pleasure, from helping that organization carry out its mission.

Keep in mind, though, the simplest way to give to a charity is by making an outright gift. You can make outright gifts either during your lifetime or at death. Donors of charitable gifts generally receive tax benefits. The availability and amount of those benefits depend on several factors.

If you want to structure the charitable gift to maximize the tax advantages, consider these factors:

- Type of property given such as cash, stock, real estate, or short-term or long-term assets
- Nature of the charitable organization
- Value and tax basis of the gift
- Your contribution base (adjusted gross income, without regard to net operating loss)
- Charitable deduction interplay between or among other charitable gifts made in the same year or "carried over" from prior tax years

I'd like to make a charitable contribution but I don't have the financial means right now. Do I have any alternatives?—Outright gifts during life can be made only by persons who can afford to do so. However, you can give to charity by using split interest trusts. These special trusts provide both a benefit to a charity and a benefit to a "non-charity"—generally the donor and the donor's family.

Split interest trusts have gained popularity because they can satisfy personal financial needs as well as philanthropic desires. The most commonly used split-interest trust is the charitable remainder trust. A less frequently used split interest trust is the charitable lead trust. Instead of getting into detail here, I suggest discussing these special trusts with an attorney who is well versed in charitable remainder trusts to see what type of trust can help you fulfill your philanthropic desires.

Personal Residence Trust

The personal residence trust is sometimes referred to as a *grantor retained income trust* (GRIT). With a GRIT, your home is transferred to an irrevocable trust for a stated period of years (usually 10 to 15). You retain the right to live in and use the home for that term of years. After that time, the home belongs to your children. In effect, you're giving your home to your children today, but they won't own it until the end of the trust. Because your children won't actually receive the home until sometime in the future, the value of the gift gets reduced or discounted. If you should die before the term of the trust is up, only the discounted value of your residence will be included in your personal estate for estate tax purposes. This uses less of your applicable exclusion amount than if you had kept your home—together with its future appreciation—in your estate.

If you live longer than the term of the trust, you may have to pay rent and upkeep on the home. Your residence won't receive a "stepped-up" basis when you die. The terms *basis* and *cost basis* describe the original purchase cost of an asset. This basis will usually increase over time. The original purchase price, or basis, will be your basis at the time of the gift. Because of this, a gain may occur on the future sale of this residence. Then, upon the sale, there will be a capital gain, so a capital gain tax will be due on the sale. Clearly it's necessary to compare the difference between the expected capital gains taxes verses estate taxes.

Under current tax law, if the owner of this residence died and passed the residence to the heirs by will or trust, the residence receives a new basis. The basis for determining a gain is now the fair market value of the residence at the time of the death of the owner (the parents).

Asset Protection Trust

If you've read John Grisham's novels, you may be familiar with asset protection trusts. But here's a news-flash: Asset protection trusts aren't just for the bad guys. In spite of all the gangsters, crooked lawyers, and dishonest businessmen who are associated with offshore dealings, bona fide, legitimate, downright honest people are associated with those tropical islands.

People in high-risk businesses or liability-intensive employment are especially interested in methods to protect their assets against judgments or lawsuits. Many of these people turn to asset protection trusts, which are purposely created in foreign countries that don't enforce judgments obtained in other jurisdictions. Some of the countries most often used for this purpose include the Isle of Man, the Cook Islands, Belize, or the Cayman Islands.

Often the person creating an asset protection trust will first create a family limited partnership. He then transfers some of the family limited partnership shares to an offshore trust. In this way, the assets themselves don't have to leave the country. If you are sued and a judgment is obtained against you, the assets are owned by your offshore trust. The judgment will have no effect in the foreign jurisdiction. To enforce the judgment, the creditor will have to seek a remedy in that foreign country. This means hiring a local attorney, sending the attorney and the witnesses to the foreign court, and many other costly inconveniences. This is usually an effective deterrent to enforcement of a judgment against your assets.

If a person's assets are transferred to such a trust after a lawsuit has been initiated or a judgment has been obtained, the transfer may be considered a transfer in defraud of creditors and may be set aside. You must establish your asset protection trust prior to such problems. Asset protection trusts may still be subject to normal income, gift, estate, excise, and business taxes. Asset protection trust planning is complicated and requires someone who is familiar with this kind of procedure.

Liquid Asset Protection Plan

Liquid asset protection plans (LAP Plans) are designed primarily to benefit those with large tax-deferred accounts such as jumbo IRAs or pension plans. These are subject at death to both an estate tax and a deferred income tax. This total tax toll can be as high as 75 percent! One of the best ways to protect these assets is by using a LAP Plan.

With a LAP Plan, spendable income is increased, income is guaranteed for life, tax-free income is distributed to the heirs at death (thus increasing the inheritance to them), and liquid assets are removed from the taxable estate, thereby reducing estate taxes. The LAP Plan works in the following manner and sequence:

Step 1—The liquid asset (for example, a jumbo IRA) is transferred to an insured tax-preferred lifetime guaranteed income annuity.

Step 2—A tax-free life insurance policy is established, using an ILIT or an FLP. This policy is outside of the taxable estate. The policy death benefit will be equal to or greater than the transferred liquid asset.

Step 3—Tax-preferred income is paid from the guaranteed annuity for the life of the transferor.

Step 4—Upon the death of the insured, the annuity income stops and the life insurance death benefit is paid to heirs outside of the taxable estate.

Repositioning the asset into the LAP Plan will:

- Increase income enough to pay all insurance costs
- Pay any income tax which may be due
- Guarantee future income
- Usually create greater spendable income for the person establishing the plan
- Remove this large asset from the taxable estate

LIQUID ASSET PROTECTION PLAN

STEP #1

Change the Forms of the Liquid Assets... to an Insured Tax Preferred Lifetime GUARANTEED income Annuity

LIQUID ASSET PROTECTION

STEP #2

Establish a Tax Free
Life Insurance Policy
*OUTSIDE OF THE
TAXABLE ESTATE*
Equal in Value to the
Transferred Asset

LIQUID ASSET PROTECTION

STEP #3

Tax- Perferred Income
is Paid from the Annuity...

...FOR AS LONG
AS YOU LIVE.

LIQUID ASSET PROTECTION

STEP #4 (Upon Death)

- Income Stops
- Insurance Pays
- Asset is Repositioned Out of the Estate!

LIQUID ASSET PROTECTION

STEP #5

LIFE INSURANCE PROCEEDS ARE:

- Received Tax Free,
- Outside the Estate,
- Invested to Provide Continuing Income to Surviving Spouse.

//

Action Items—Chapter 8: Keeping Assets Safe from Lawsuits, Creditors and Judgments

Action 1: Review the trusts discussed in this chapter. Which ones could benefit you and your family? Refer to this checklist when you contact an estate planning attorney:

❑ Family Limited Partnership
❑ Irrevocable Life Insurance Trust
❑ Charitable Remainder Trust
❑ Personal Residence Trust
❑ Asset Protection Trust
❑ Liquid Asset Protection Plan

Go to *www.EstatePlanningDr.com/book* to download:

Checklist of Asset Protection Tools

//

Chapter Nine

What If You're Not Rich but Still Want Protection?

People often ask if their assets are protected simply by having them listed in their revocable living trust. The answer is *"No!"* Since you have the right to alter, amend, or even revoke your trust, the law says that the assets in your trust are subject to your creditors as if no trust existed. Yet you want your assets to be safe from lawsuits, creditors, and possible court judgments. What's the answer?

Well, the best liability protection is to own no assets. Be destitute. Flat broke. Impoverished. In such a condition, you would be judgment proof simply because "you can't get blood from a turnip." But no one wants to be poverty stricken to avoid liability. It's an absurd suggestion—and an uncomfortable situation. Fortunately, you can avoid losing your assets without divesting yourself of everything you own.

Why would you want to become judgment proof? The number-one reason is the desire to avoid unreasonable or frivolous lawsuits that have begun to run rampant in our society. In our litigious society, being served with a lawsuit is no longer the exception, it's the rule. Statistics show that one in four people in the United States will be sued this year.

Beyond that, you may wish to keep a comfortable estate for your own succor and support. If you aren't wealthy but are getting by on your own reserves, you may still wish to avoid the required spend-down should you need to apply for Medicaid or other assistance from the government.

What do I mean by *spend-down*? The government rules relating to Medicaid assistance in the event of your need seem as though they were written only for those educated in this area. Simply stated, the rules require that you must be impoverished to get assistance. Therefore, if you have too many items of value, you must spend your own money for your medical assistance—at least until you arrive at the point of being considered poor enough for government help.

Yes, you may be required to sell some of your valuable assets. You may keep your personal residence. Even when you're in an assisted living facility, you may keep your home if you intend to return to it someday. You may also keep your car in most cases. When you reach the point of "impoverishment," then you may be entitled to government assistance and you'll need to apply with the appropriate agency in your state.

When you die, the state will recover as much money from your estate as it can to reimburse the state for the cost of your assistance. Even assets you were allowed to keep—such as your house and car—will be subject to estate recovery. If you receive government assistance, you may wish to avoid the mandated estate recovery.

Keep in mind that Medicaid is a federal program that each individual state administers. The federal government mandates that each state must seek to recover as much of its Medicaid expenditures as possible. For example, let's say that Mr. Brown received Medicaid funds from the state. Upon Mr. Brown's death, the state has the responsibility to recover as much as possible—up to the dollar amount of the assistance—from Mr. Brown's estate. This is known as *estate recovery*. The state can place a Medicaid lien upon the estate of the decedent, which must be paid before the estate can be distributed to the family or other heirs. This lien applies to assets that were previously not counted, such as your residence and automobile.

> ## "I Can't Believe They Took Her House!"
>
> It was a tough day when my client Joan Vincent sat across my desk and, with an absent-minded stare, kept repeating, "I can't believe they took her house!" Joan's mother, Mrs. Vincent, had just lost her house to the state. In the last few years of her life, Mrs. Vincent had been assisted by Medicaid. At the time of her death, all she had left to her name was her residence, which she had hoped to pass on to her two children. The week after Mrs. Vincent died, Joan hired me to re-title her mother's home. When I went to file the Affidavit for the Transfer of Real Property, the registrar informed me that the affidavit couldn't be filed. The state of Arizona had already recorded a Medicaid lien against the property. I've never seen the government move so quickly!
>
> Now, Mrs. Vincent's house had to be sold—with the proceeds going to the government. She may have been able to avoid this sad situation with a little planning.

Many people think their estate is too small to require estate planning. Others don't plan because they don't know where to turn for help. Some people believe the only financial protection for their old age is expensive, long-term care insurance. In fact, the number-one concern for many senior citizens is their possible need for long-term care assistance and how to avoid impoverishment should that happen. Although each estate is different, everyone can avoid the Medicaid trap and the effects of federally mandated estate recovery. It just takes a little planning.

Medicaid Annuity

Annuities have become a popular way to protect your assets in the event of a catastrophic illness. When you apply for government assistance, you must list all your real estate, bank accounts, stocks and bonds, and so on. Since an annuity is a contract between you and your insurance company, the government considers it a *noncountable asset*. That means you won't have to spend down the principal to qualify for government assistance.

For example, let's say you have a $50,000 certificate of deposit with your bank. Unexpectedly, you need long-term medical assistance or need to be placed in a nursing home. You apply for government help but the government agency says you don't qualify for help because your net worth is too high. You must first spend that $50,000 CD and then reapply for government assistance.

Let's assume you transfer that same $50,000 to a Medicaid-qualifying annuity. You can still receive the income from that annuity and you don't have to spend the $50,000 before receiving government assistance. Most annuities even have withdrawal provisions that allow you to take a part of the principal without penalty. However, your annuity must follow the Medicaid guidelines to be acceptable.

Caution: Congress has recently passed legislation restricting the use of Medicaid-qualifying annuities. You must work with an experienced elder law attorney for assistance in such matters.

How Annuities Work

A Medicaid-qualifying annuity is an agreement or contract between you and an insurance company. You agree to transfer certain funds to the insurance company and the insurance company agrees to pay you a certain amount either over a fixed period of time or over your lifetime. Your funds are safe. The insurance company promises a guaranteed return or interest on your investment. You're entitled to receive only the agreed-upon distribution amount. However, you may withdraw funds, subject to certain restrictions (these restrictions tend to be less restrictive than a certificate of deposit with a bank).

You're no longer considered the owner of the principal that was transferred to your annuity. Because the funds transferred to the insurance company are no longer owned by you, they're no longer in your estate. In effect, this method converts a countable asset to an income stream. All countable assets are totaled to determine if your assets exceed the established value to qualify for government assistance. Therefore, having that $50,000—if you place it in an annuity and it's no longer a countable asset—won't disqualify you from receiving government benefits in the event of a catastrophic illness. And you can try to qualify for Medicaid assistance without having to spend down your assets to meet the monetary requirements.

The annuity contract insures against the risk you live so long that you outlive your funds. It protects you from using up your estate before your death. The annuity usually pays you or accumulates a greater interest on your money than you would have received from your bank certificate of deposit.

Fundamentally, a Medicaid annuity is an immediate annuity that meets the requirement described by the Centers for Medicare and Medicaid Services (a federal agency within the United States Department of Health and Human Services), which sets the standards and guidelines for Medicaid. But be careful. Not all immediate annuities meet these guidelines. And no insurance company issues a clearly designated "Medicaid annuity." Deal with a reputable agent or elder law attorney to make certain your annuity will meet these standards.

Also, consider an annuity if you're going to receive lump-sum distributions from tax-deferred employee benefit plans, IRAs, or KEOGH plans. When used together with irrevocable life insurance trusts (also called *wealth replacement insurance trusts*) and charitable giving trusts, annuities may produce highly desirable results.

//

Action Items—Chapter 9: What If You're Not Rich but Still Want Protection?

I offer the proverbial "wake-up call." Don't wait! Don't leave open the possibility of your children saying, "I can't believe they took the house!"

Action 1: Gather all the information concerning your estate.—Review this information to discover which assets are exposed to estate recovery.

Action 2: Determine which methods you could use to best protect those assets.—The three most popular methods are: Medicaid annuity, family limited partnership, and asset protection trusts.

Go to *www.EstatePlanningDr.com/book* to download:

Schedule of Assets Analysis Form

//

Chapter Ten

"If I Own a Business, How Can I Protect My Assets from Creditors, Predators, and Probate?"

I'm constantly amazed how many people are in business for themselves but don't pay attention to the best way to organize their businesses. Doctors, dentists, professional speakers, and owners of multilevel marketing businesses seem to be especially neglectful of this. What do I mean by this? When people start a business, they often don't consider the best type of business entity to use to get the most out of business-tax deductions, protect their business and personal assets, and pass the business on to their heirs in the event of death or incapacity. Believe it or not, business planning is a critical part of estate planning—and estate planning is an essential component of business planning!

I congratulate you if you've already considered your business to be a part of your estate plan. If you have yet to take care of these issues, take note of the tips that follow.

Over the years, I've compiled information to help my clients understand the pros and cons of different types of business entities: sole proprietorships, general partnerships, C-corporations, subchapter-S corporations, and the relatively new entity, limited liability companies (LLCs). Each entity is different and gets treated differently for tax purposes. This chapter presents an overview to determine which type of business entity would be the best for you.

Protect Your Personal Assets!

Be sure to keep your business and investment assets separate from your personal assets. Don't ever let your personal assets subject your business to creditors' claims.

Sole Proprietorship

This is the most basic form of doing business. As one tax analyst puts it, "You keep all the profits and accept the entire risk of loss. It is capitalism at its most basic." Sole proprietorship is best for small businesses and businesses in their early start-up phases. Details on this type of business entity follow.

How complicated is it to create and operate a sole proprietorship?—You don't need to take formal action; you merely start doing business. However, your municipality or state might require various licenses, depending on the nature of the business and where you're operating it.

What tax issues should I consider?—You report business profits or losses on your individual tax return. On Schedule C, you list business income and take deductions for expenses. The net profit is taxed at personal income tax rates (federal rates range from 15 to 39.6 percent). If you lose money, you can't deduct losses but can carry them forward to the next tax year. If you make a profit that next year, you deduct the losses accrued from the previous year (or years) from your profit. However, you can't reduce your net business income to less than zero.

Would my assets be at risk if I'm found liable for a problem?—You are personally liable for every business debt, just as if you had incurred such liabilities as personal expenses. That means all your personal and business assets are at risk.

How easy is it to raise money?—Most banks and other lending entities will require personal collateral (home equity or other valuables). Too often, capital is generated only from your personal resources—by borrowing on credit cards or from family members.

What happens to my business if I sell, become disabled, or die?—You have no separately existing business entity. Thus, if you die or become incapacitated, your business goes with you. Selling is a bit more feasible—but only if you have an established service business or a readily assumed, product-based business. For these reasons, estate planning becomes vital for sole proprietors.

General Partnership

You create a general partnership structure by an agreement. It can be an oral agreement but should be in writing. To avoid unnecessary troubles, it's wise to solicit the aid of an attorney. Your agreement should set forth the respective ownership interests of the partners, the extent of each partner's investment in the business, and other important matters. As LLC companies become more popular, general partnerships seem to be growing obsolete.

How complicated is it to create and operate a partnership?—Because you must address so many terms in the agreement—including the rights and obligations of each partner, what happens if a partner dies, and so forth—a partnership can be more complicated than it might initially appear. With so much to consider, have a lawyer advise you on the issues and prepare and negotiate the agreement. Problems can arise when partners have differing views of how the business should operate or think that one partner is doing more work than the other.

What tax issues should I consider?—Although it isn't taxed as a single entity, total profit and losses are tallied for the business. Each partner then files an individual tax return (using Schedule K-1) that includes the amount of that partner's respective tax liability and is taxed accordingly. For example, setting up a retirement plan becomes complicated because, if all partners can't agree on the type of plan, it might be impossible to have a plan.

Would my assets be at risk if I'm found liable for a problem?—Each partner is personally responsible for all the business liabilities of the partnership and even for the individual liabilities incurred by other partners during the course of partnership activities. Each partner's personal assets are potentially at risk. If a bill isn't paid, you can be made to pay the entire amount if your partners are unable to pay their respective shares.

How easy is it to raise money?—Partners contribute time, money, or property to receive equity interest. These contributions must be tracked and will have ramifications for each partner. Borrowing from banks or other lending sources can be as problematic as for sole proprietors; personal collateral often is necessary.

What happens to my business if I sell, become disabled, or die?—In the partnership agreement, partners can provide for the contingency of another's death, incapacity, or desire to sell his equity. One option is setting up a buy/sell agreement. You can agree as partners that upon a partner's death, the deceased partner's heirs will receive the proceeds of a life insurance policy. (You would take out such policies for the purpose of buying out the interest of the deceased partner.) In return, the heirs will lose all rights, title, and interest in the partnership business. Otherwise you may remain a partner with your deceased partner's spouse or other heirs.

C-Corporation

By incorporating your business, you create an entity that is separate and distinct from you as an individual. Special laws and taxes apply to any corporation. A C-corporation (the standard type) may not be the best structure for a small business, especially one in start-up phase. The formalities are many and the tax consequences may leave less money in your pocket. It's interesting that the tax on the first $50,000 of net income is taxed at a rate of 15 percent, which may also provide some tax benefits.

The liability protection you might seek in a C-corporation can also be found in a limited-liability company or a sub-chapter-S corporation. However, if your business is growing large and you want to raise money through the sale of stock, a C-corporation may be the way to go.

How complicated is it to create and operate a C-corporation?—To incorporate, you must file articles of incorporation, create corporate bylaws, and fulfill other state requirements. You must issue stock, even if you're the sole shareholder. If you commingle personal and corporate assets or otherwise fail to conduct the corporation as a separate and distinct entity, you may lose your right to limited liability—which is a primary reason for forming a corporation. However, on a personal judgment against a corporate shareholder, the stock may be subject to attachment by the creditor.

What tax issues should I consider?—Your business must report income on a corporate tax return, separate from shareholders' returns. Also, regardless of profitability, many states have minimum taxes that corporations must pay. Shareholders will be taxed for dividends received and, of course, any salaries from your corporation will be taxed at individual rates. Corporate tax returns are more complicated than individual returns, which generally translates to paying higher fees to a tax professional. On the other hand, corporations are usually taxed at a slightly lower rate than individuals—15 percent on the first $50,000 of the taxable income, and then 34 percent maximum (versus 39.6 percent). In addition, a C-corporation may select a tax year, or fiscal year, ending in a month other than December.

Would my assets be at risk if I'm found liable for a problem?—Limited liability for shareholders is a vital benefit. Under normal circumstances, a corporate owner's liability is limited to funds invested in the stock. Stockholders can't be held personally liable for corporate actions and creditors are limited to corporate assets when seeking to collect monies owed.

How easy is it to raise money?—Corporations have a method of raising money not available to other types of business structures: They sell stock to the public. Furthermore, standard C-corporations don't limit who can own stock or the number of shareholders, thereby maximizing the potential access to capital.

What happens to my business if I sell, become disabled, or die?—Once formed, a corporation continues in existence until it is formally shut down. Thus, if a key player in the corporation dies, formal action isn't required by the corporation to deal with the problem. The percentage ownership of the deceased will simply pass to the heirs. Also, under most circumstances, stockholders can sell their stock whenever and to whomever they please. As a shareholder, you should consider the corporate stock in your overall estate plan. It's best to hold the stock in the name of the shareholder's revocable living trust.

Subchapter-S Corporation

To combine corporate liability protection with the tax aspects of a partnership, consider this popular structure: subchapter-S corporation (also called *small business corporation*). There are, however, restrictions as to who may participate, which can be problematic when raising capital. For example, in addition to the restriction on the number of shareholders, foreign nationals may not hold subchapter-S stock.

As a shareholder, you should consider the corporate stock of an S-corporation in your overall estate plan. It's best to hold the stock in the name of the shareholder's revocable living trust. This means the living trust must have qualifying S-corporation language.

How complicated is it to create and operate a subchapter-S corporation?—Creating a subchapter-S corporation is about as complicated as forming a standard C-corporation.

What tax issues should I consider?—Shareholders are taxed as if they're in a partnership and file individual rather than corporate tax returns. The fiscal year for an S-Corporation must be a calendar year (year ending in December).

Would my assets be at risk if I'm found liable for a problem?—As with a C-corporation, you have no stockholder liability beyond the assets of the corporation. However, on a personal judgment against a corporate shareholder of an S-corporation, the stock may be subject to attachment by the creditor.

How easy is it to raise money?—A subchapter-S corporation can have up to 75 stockholders. That enhances its ability to raise working capital. However, if you wish to offer shares to investors at large, you will need to form a standard C-corporation.

What happens to my business if I sell, become disabled, or die?—A subchapter-S corporation offers the same flexibility as a C-corporation.

Limited Liability Company

This relatively new business structure can be formed in any of the 50 states. A limited liability company (LLC) has the limited liability of a corporation but the flexibility and tax status of a partnership. That makes it an up-and-comer in business circles.

How complicated is it to create and operate an LLC?—You must file this business entity with the appropriate state authorities. Usually this consists of the articles of organization and the operating agreement. It's important to dot all the "i"s and cross all the "t"s when creating this structure. Therefore, you should retain an attorney who understands the laws in your state.

What tax issues should I consider?—LLCs can be taxed four different ways and you get to select the way. They are:

1. Choose your LLC to be a disregarded entity. In that case, you would be taxed as a sole proprietor.
2. Have your LLC taxed as a partnership. In this case, you report profits and losses on a personal, rather than corporate, tax return.
3. Select to be taxed as an S-corporation.
4. Select to be taxed as a C-corporation.

Would my assets be at risk if I'm found liable for a problem?—As the name implies, liability is limited to the assets of the limited liability company.

How easy is it to raise money?—The restrictions on securing capital are the same as those of a general partnership. Your revenue options are limited because you can't raise money through shareholders.

What happens to my business if I sell, become disabled, or die?—You'll have to engage in succession planning, as you would in a general partnership.

Which Business Entity is Right for You?

If you own a small business and wish to have some degree of asset protection but still want the benefits of tax deductions and pass-through taxation—that is, you don't want to pay a corporate tax and an additional tax as the shareholder of the company—then you'd select small business corporation (subchapter-S corporation) status for tax purposes. That means you're treated like a business entity and get the limited liability. Plus, after your many business deductions, the net income is passed through to you as an individual and you report the business net income on your personal tax return. You don't have the double taxation as for a C-corporation and you'll still have many tax deductions and other benefits.

Talk to your accountant for the corporate deductions for which you're entitled. One accountant I know had a list of approximately 300 business deductions for a corporation—deductions that aren't available to a sole proprietor.

Also, as a small business corporation, you're not subject to self-employment tax for all the business net income. (Self-employment tax would subject all your income to Social Security withholding.) With this corporation, you may take a salary as an employee, which is subject to the FICA (Social Security) tax, but the net income over and above your salary and other corporate expenses may be passed on to the shareholders without this FICA tax. This can represent a substantial savings in many cases.

This subchapter-S corporation works particularly well for professionals such as speakers, photographers, and real estate agents. Plus, licensed professionals (such as dentists, doctors, and lawyers) must select professional corporation status. Only the licensed professional may own stock in such a corporation.

Remember that your stock is still subject to probate if you're the business owner. That's why you need a revocable living trust; it would own the stock for you and you would avoid probate. If you're a licensed professional, you'll need to have a professional corporation trust to hold your shares of stock.

To incorporate, you would file your Articles of Incorporation with your state's corporation commission and publish your Articles for the number of times directed by your state's laws on incorporating. You would print stock certificates and create a corporate record book to keep records of your Articles, adopted by-laws, stock transfer ledger, and your minutes of the annual meetings of the shareholders and the board of directors.

Note that you must hold annual meetings of shareholders and directors at least once a year. The shareholders own the company and elect the directors of the corporation and approve past activities of the directors. The directors nominate the officers of the company, including its president, any vice presidents, secretary, and treasurer, and any other positions the directors determine. You must keep minutes of any unusual or major decisions of the shareholders and directors. You'll be required to file the annual report as directed by the laws of your state.

You might ask: Why do I have to file all these reports and keep records? Because if you don't treat your company like a separate entity—like a business—no one else will. If you don't have such records and you get sued, the courts may set aside your corporate status and allow judgments to be taken against you individually. That means you could lose your corporate asset protection. The IRS may also treat you as though you had no separate business corporation and disallow your business deductions.

Keep Good Records

Many people elect to simplify their business entity by using the relatively new business entity called the *limited liability company*. The LLC has filing requirements similar to a corporation to get started. However, it's more flexible and has fewer filing requirements. No annual reports are required so you wouldn't incur an annual filing fee. However, you must still keep good business records, including minutes of meetings. Sad to say, many people start their new LLC and neglect to keep any records. What happens to your company if it gets sued or audited? If you don't keep business records, the LLC business entity may be ignored for asset protection or for tax benefits. Be careful!

215

The LLC is an excellent business choice if you have more than one owner and if one owner is the business-savvy partner, another partner is the product developer, and another partner brings the money to get the company off the ground. The LLC operating agreement, which is necessary, can define everyone's relationship to the business. Therefore, the LLC is much more flexible than the corporation, which is controlled by the vote of the shareholders. It's governed by its operating agreement. Consider using this business entity if you intend to grow your business or take on new partners. But keep good records!

For tax purposes, the LLC may elect to be treated as a corporation or as a partnership. Talk this over carefully with your accountant. If you elect to be treated as a partnership, you may still be subject to the self-employment tax (the FICA tax). If you wish to be treated as a pass-through entity, such as a subchapter-S corporation, then you may elect to be treated as a corporation for tax purposes and then choose small-business corporation (subchapter-S corporation) status.

//

Action Items—Chapter 10: If I Own a Business, How Can I Protect My Assets from Creditors, Predators, and Probate?

Do you own a business? If so, take time to complete the following actions to determine the type of business entity that would help make your business successful, get the most out of business-tax deductions, and protect your business and personal assets from creditors, predators, and probate.

Action 1: Select the type of business entity that works best for you.—Consider your business activities, need for liability protection, current and future partnerships, future investment needs, and how you would pass on your business to your heirs.

Action 2: Locate a good business attorney.—Always ask a lot of questions. Ensure the attorney has experience establishing business entities and creating asset protection for various business entities including partnerships, C-corporations, subchapter-S corporations, and limited liability companies. And make sure the attorney knows how to make your business part of your estate plan.

Go to *www.EstatePlanningDr.com/book* to download:

Corporate Entity Schedule and Worksheet

//

Chapter Eleven

Track Your Business Deductions and Give Yourself a Raise

Y ou can't leave an estate behind for your heirs if you don't have one. Part of estate planning, then, is building your nest egg. The importance of building wealth to take care of your personal needs, your business needs, your health requirements, and the needs of your retirement (beginning with your "financial freedom day") cannot be overstated.

Do you track your business deductions? Do you take full advantage of the business deductions to which you're legitimately entitled? Have you found your own qualified CPA to help you strategize and plan ahead—not just to fill out tax forms? With expert guidance, you may be pleasantly surprised at how much you can save in taxes. After consulting with one client and teaching him the basic rules of legitimate tax deductions, he saved more than $10,000 in taxes in one year. My daughter who makes jewelry applied these principles and saved $5,000 one year. Ecstatic, she said: "Dad, over the next five years, you'll have helped me save $25,000!"

Some may say, "She didn't actually get a raise. She just found a way to save on taxes. She still received the same amount of income." Yes, that's true. But consider this: If you're going to purchase an item anyway, isn't it better to purchase that item with pretax dollars instead of with dollars that have been or will be taxed?" If you purchase an item with dollars that won't be taxed, isn't that like getting a raise?

Consider Starting a Home-Based Business to Increase Wealth

Setting up a home-based business can jumpstart your wealth plan because it'll dramatically reduce your taxes. This truism is an interesting anomaly. If you're employed by a company other than your own, you know your total annual wage and you know your take-home pay for each pay period. You may not often consider that these two amounts don't reconcile. Have you paid much attention to that huge amount withheld from your paycheck in the form of tax withholding?

The government learned years ago that taxpayers don't squeal when a little tax is withheld from paychecks and sent to Uncle Sam each payday. Most taxpayers hardly notice this. But if these same taxpayers had to pay the withheld amount in one lump-sum on tax day each year, they might protest and hold another Boston Tea Party!

The largest number of taxpayers is W-2 wage earners who receive paychecks and then pay their bills, buy necessities, splurge on extras, squirrel away a bit into savings, give to charities, and take vacations. They do all this with after-tax money—money that came to them after the taxes were withheld from their paychecks.

Many people who own their own businesses (whether large or small) are educated taxpayers—they see gargantuan reductions in their tax loads thanks to the number of allowed deductions for business owners.

Businesses have at least 85 legal, proper deductions that wage-earners don't have access to. Corporations have as many as 300. Under our tax system, businesses may deduct costs for transportation, health care, meals, home office, child care, and other items business owners would have to buy for personal use if they weren't used in their businesses.

Imagine how speedily you could move along on your path to wealth if you could keep a significant portion of the 25 to 50 percent of your earned income you give to Uncle Sam in withholding taxes!

Go to Work or Create a Home-Based Business? Let's Do the Math

A 1994 article in *Woman's Day* magazine by Jane Bryant Quinn presented an excellent comparison between a wage-earner and a small business owner. This article, "How to Live on One Salary," assumed that the husband earned $40,000 a year and his wife, referred to as Lori, was a stay-at-home mom. This couple, like many others, had "more month than money." Lori decided to take a corporate administration job paying $15,000 a year. The couple was startled when they closely examined the *negative* financial effects that her job had on their household income.

Because they were married, they filed jointly on their combined income. Lori would now pay $4,500 in new federal and state income tax, most of which they could not deduct. The mandatory Social Security withholding tax from Lori's paycheck (7.65 percent) meant an additional $1,158 was withheld from her income. Lori's ten-mile commute to work resulted in an additional $696 in nondeductible expenses. (Remember, this article was written in 1994; this amount might be twice that today!)

Placing their child in day care created an annual expense of $4,250. Lori ate lunch with coworkers at local eateries, which added a nondeductible expense of $1,250. And her new job required professional clothing and, subsequently, additional dry-cleaning expenses. Quinn's article assumed these expenses to be about $1,000 a year. Again, nondeductible.

Now that Lori's life was busier, she cooked fewer meals from scratch and the family ate out more often, resulting in an increase of food costs estimated at $1,000 a year.

Taking all these expenses into account, Lori's take-home pay was only $1,156 a year! For this meager sum, Lori had to deal with the commute and the hassles that came with her job.

Quinn compared these figures with a new scenario: Lori starts her own business. In this scenario, Lori becomes an administrative consultant and starts her own home-based business.

She would not need to spend any more money than she was currently spending. She would have the same food and transportation expenses, yet many of these expenses would become business deductions. By tracking legal, proper deductions and assuming an honest expectation of profit, Lori would keep the entire $15,000 she made as income, thanks to her business deductions.

No wonder the United States has seen an estimated 20-fold increase in the number of new home-based businesses started in the past 10 years!

What kind of home-based business is right for you? Well, what are good at? What types of projects, skills, or tasks are interesting or exciting to you—activities that you could offer to other people for a fee? Consider your past work experience as well as your hobbies.

Keep in mind that new businesses become successful when business owners apply *action* and *knowledge*. If you want to take advantage of owning your own business, you must take action in your areas of skills or knowledge that will be marketable. This will bring the desired results.

You'll need to decide the type of business entity to use such as a sole proprietorship or subchapter-S corporation discussed earlier. This is a personal choice, depending on the type of business, number of parties involved, asset protection requirements, desired flexibility, and many other factors. However, don't delay this important decision in the interest of quickly getting your new business up and running. Refer to Chapter Ten for a refresher course on the pros and cons of different business entities.

Learn the Basic Rules of Tax Deductions

A married couple, Mr. and Mrs. Author, are both technical writers, work for themselves, and are semi-retired. The Authors spoke to me about a revocable living trust they had set up nine years before. When they read over their trust agreement, they found confusing language. Some components were even called by different names in different paragraphs. It just wasn't clear. They wanted to understand their trust to make sure it met their needs. Several times they had even called the attorney who had prepared the trust but he never returned their calls. The Authors got my name from a friend of theirs.

After reviewing and discussing their needs with them, I helped them decide to create a new trust. When I advised them to keep the original name and signing date of their trust, they agreed. That would eliminate transferring the assets already in their trust and, as a result, save some confusion.

Next, we reviewed the assets in their estate to determine which ones needed to be titled in or transferred to their trust. When we came to the limited liability company that they'd established for their business, we discovered they hadn't connected their membership interest in their LLC to their trust. I advised them to have the LLC membership interest held in their trust and reminded them of the importance of holding regular board meetings.

When I asked Mr. and Mrs. Author what type of tax entity they had chosen for their LLC, they admitted that they didn't know. After a few questions, I determined that their LLC was taxed as a disregarded entity. That meant all their income was considered self-employment income subject to Social Security (FICA) tax. And they said those seven deadly words: "My accountant takes care of my taxes."

The Authors were surprised when I suggested reconsidering the type of tax entity they had chosen by default. If they converted to small business corporation status (subchapter-S corporation), they might save on their taxes. Not all their income needed to be self-employment income.

I asked if they ever went on vacations. The Authors replied, "Of course we do." They were taken aback when I suggested they should never take another vacation. "But we need and enjoy our vacations," they argued. I reminded them that they're supposed to have an annual meeting of the members of their LLC to discuss its operation and business activities. Such a meeting can be held anywhere in the continental United States. It's a proper business expense.

As writers, they could take a trip and find a business purpose for such an adventure. They could go to places related to their writing, for example, visit publishing companies or even libraries. These costs and expenses can become business deductions.

Also, they used the study in their home as their office but didn't take the home office deduction. They didn't know that Congress had passed laws allowing certain benefits if you work from home. Their identifiable home office area qualifies as a principal place of business because they use this area to conduct administrative and management activities; there is no other place where they conduct substantial administrative activities.

They agreed that they had an identifiable area of their home used solely for those purposes. Plus, they meet with clients in their home for business reasons from time to time and have to make sure their home is presentable. We discussed that their lawn maintenance and home cleaning services might be business expenses. They should also have a home security system to protect their important business records.

Next, I reminded them of the importance of keeping good company records, corporate minutes, and expense records. They needed a separate book of their LLC board meeting minutes. They should create an operating agreement for their company and a ledger listing the members of their company. If they were audited and hadn't maintained good business records, they could be in trouble. I stressed this important point: *If they didn't treat their LLC like a business, the IRS wouldn't either.* And if they happened to be sued by a creditor or predator, a lawyer could "pierce the corporate veil." Their personal assets wouldn't be protected. Remember, this is a key reason to set up a separate business entity.

Next, we discussed automobile use, meals out of and in the home, supplies, and other expenses that could be business uses. I advised them to become educated about taxes. Their accountant would not always tell them how to take advantage of the deductions that could easily be theirs. But they needed to properly document these new expenses. They'd benefit from having a computer system and accounting program to keep track of their financial records. It would help them to work with an accountant who can identify appropriate deductions, not someone who simply tallies receipts and completes their tax returns.

Expect more from your CPA! Find an accountant who will meet with you during the year to plan your activities—not just at year end when it's too late to plan ahead and the accountant is too frantic with the upcoming tax season. When you own a small business, becoming knowledgeable about taxes, deductions, and planning ahead is especially important.

After we met, I gave the Authors this homework:

- List your ten largest expenses, then ask, "Which of these expenses, if recorded properly, would relate to our business?"
- Change the way you think about purchases, then ask, "How can we purchase products or services in the future to have a business relationship and take advantage of those deductions?"

You would appreciate a raise right now, wouldn't you? Follow the action items below to get organized, take your legitimate deductions, and reduce your taxable income. In short, give yourself a raise!

//

Action Items—Chapter 11: Track Your Business Deductions and Give Yourself a Raise

Action 1: Become educated on tax deductions. I recommend Sandy Botkin's audio CDs: *Tax Strategies for Business Professionals—A Simple and Easy Guide to Reduce and Audit-Proof Taxes.* (Sandy Botkin is a CPA, a former IRS attorney, and senior tax law specialist.)

Action 2: If you're into real estate, become educated on its tax implications. I recommend Sandy Botkin's *Wealth Building Tax Secrets for Real Estate.*

Action 3: Keep good records. Consider using the *Tax Reduction Organizer—The Easy Way to 'Audit Proof' Your Entertainment, Fun, Travel, Etc.* by the Tax Reduction Institute.

Action 4: Discipline yourself to hold quarterly board meetings. At a minimum you must hold annual meetings. Be sure to keep written minutes of each meeting. Place your minutes in a special Corporate or LLC Record Book.

If you are not sure how to prepare these minutes, or would like to have them prepared for you, go to *www. JustAMinuteLLC.com.* This is a company that will do that for you. And at a reasonable expense (much less than a lawyer).

229

Go to *www.estatePlanningDr.com/book* to download:

Links to Sandy Botkin's products

Link to JustAMinute corporate minutes services.

A fool-proof way to keeping your corporate minutes up-to-date.

//

Chapter Twelve

How to Link Your Business Entities to Your Estate Plan

If you own a business such as a limited liability company, subchapter-S corporation, or C-corporation, you must remain on guard. Each business entity must be properly included in your overall estate plan. Link your business entities with your living trust for maximum protection. Your living trust is the foundation of your estate plan and everything else will be a building block on your trust. Review all your entities to ensure they work in your overall plan. Work with your estate planning attorney to learn how your entities will be affected and how they'll relate to your trust.

Don't hesitate to talk in depth with your attorney about linking your businesses with your living trust. Because everyone's situation is different, it's difficult to offer specific instructions in this book regarding the correct way to title each entity in your unique trust.

Three Steps to Safeguard Your New Business

After you've created and signed your living trust, remember these basic steps when you create your new business entity.

Step 1: Certificates—If you're creating an LLC, your membership interest in your new LLC should be issued in the name of your trust, with you as trustee. For example: The Celebrity Trust, John Doe, Trustee. If you're creating a corporation, stock certificates from the new corporation (subchapter-S corporation or C-corporation) should be issued in the name of your trust, with you as trustee. If you're creating a limited partnership, certificates should also be issued to the name of your trust, with you as trustee.

Step 2: Ledgers—If you're creating an LLC or limited partnership, make sure the schedule of membership interests shows that your interest is held by you as trustee of your trust. If you're creating a corporation, make sure the corporate stock transfer ledger shows your interest is held by you as trustee of your trust.

Step 3: Trust schedule—If you have a trust, list your membership interest or stock certificate shares on your trust schedule under the headings of *Corporations* or *Limited Partnerships*. You should be able to find your trust schedule in your living trust binder behind the trust agreement itself. If your schedule doesn't have a subhead of *Corporations* or *Limited Partnerships*, then add this.

How to Transfer Existing Business Entities to Your Trust

Corporations are owned by shareholders who are issued stock certificates representing their ownership interest. When you have a trust, your stock certificates should show the trust as the owner. If you already have an existing corporation and if you have the corporate minute book, you should cancel your original stock certificate and issue a new one to yourself as trustee of your trust. Update the stock transfer ledger to indicate this ownership change. If you don't have a stock certificate or a stock transfer ledger, see a business attorney to have this corrected.

Limited liability companies are owned by members. Most LLCs don't have certificates of ownership (such as stock certificates in a corporation); instead, they have a schedule of ownership interests, which indicates the percentage (or share) of ownership. Be sure you update this schedule of ownership interests to show that your interest in the LLC is now owned by you as trustee of your trust. Some attorneys prefer to issue unit certificates to indicate the ownership share. This isn't a bad idea—it'll readily show your interest is owned by your trust.

Family limited partnerships are much like LLCs. However, their ownership interest is usually represented by units of partnership interest, much like a stock certificate. These should also be reissued in the name of the trust. Be sure the Schedule of Partnership Interests reflects that the partnership interests are held in the name of the trust. The partnership interest should be listed on the trust Schedule of Assets.

To transfer existing business entities to your trust, you need to take the following actions:

1. Issue the certificate showing the number of units of partnership interest in the name of the trust.

2. Make sure the schedule of partnership interests shows that the respective interests have been issued in the name of the trust.

3. Make sure the schedule of trust assets for the trust lists the partnership interests as an asset of the trust.

What About Bank Accounts?

Don't change bank accounts for your business, whether they're corporations, LLCs, family partnerships, or other business entities. Bank accounts continue to be held by the business itself, which is now owned by the trust.

How to Sign Your Documents When You Have a Living Trust

When you sign documents as the trustee on behalf of a revocable living trust, it should be clearly indicated. Sign checks on checking accounts held in the name of the trust with your name followed by a comma and the word *Trustee*. Legal documents on behalf of the trust should be prepared with this in mind.

The signature line will look like this:

The Genesis Trust, under Agreement dated 1-15-07
By_____
Jacob Alexander, Trustee

However, when acting on behalf of your business entity, you'll simply sign on behalf of that business entity as an officer or manager. You don't need to reference your trust.

By_____
Jacob Alexander
President, XYZ Company, LLC

Action Items—Chapter 12: How to Link Your Business Entities to Your Estate Plan

Follow these three easy steps to link your business entities to your trust. When you do, your businesses may continue to operate properly even in the event of your death or incapacity. Your successor trustee will simply step into your shoes and keep your business secure.

Action 1: Check that your stock or membership certificates are titled correctly. — Make sure that your corporate stock or LLC certificate of membership interest shows the owner is you as trustee of your trust. If it doesn't, issue new certificates.

Action 2: Be sure your entity ledgers are titled correctly.—If your business is a corporation, make sure your corporate stock transfer ledger shows your interest is being held by you as trustee of your trust. If it doesn't, correct the ledger. If your business is an LLC or partnership, make sure that the schedule of membership interests (commonly titled *Exhibit B: Percentage Interests of Members*) shows your interest is being held by you as trustee of your trust. Again, if it doesn't, correct the ledger.

Action 3: Ensure your entity is listed on your living trust schedule.—Make sure your corporation or LLC is listed as an asset of your trust. On your revocable living trust's list of trust property, you should describe any corporate stock, LLC membership interest, or partnership interest that you own.

Go to *www.EstatePlanningDr.com/book* to download:
• A special report on how to do this yourself
• Find out how to get professional assistance if needed

Chapter Thirteen
_____

Something for Doctors to Consider

(special recommendations for Doctors, Dentists and Licensed Professionals)

Many of my clients are coctors or dentists. It's a wonderful thing. As a general rule, they are very good at what they do and are pleasant to work with. They are intelligent, educated, and ambitious. Because of their status in the community, it is sometimes difficult to get their attention and have them consider the impact their death would have on their family, their assets, and especially their business.

Often a doctor or other professional will conduct his business through a business entity, such as a professional corporation or limited liability company. They, of course, do this to take advantage of the many business and tax benefits from such a process.

Malpractice insurance is becoming a very real and burdensome obligation in such a business. If sued at law, a doctor's business and personal assets are at risk. For this reason many professionals will conduct their business from a professional corporation.

In addition the professional may have several other entities. He may have one entity to own the equipment used in the practice, another entity to own the land or building from which the business is conducted. Then he may have still other entities to protect investment assets. These may include other LLCs, corporations, asset protection trusts, or family limited partnerships.

If a doctor's business is incorporated there are special circumstances which have to be considered. If a doctor dies his business comes to a standstill. It loses its value quickly.

Using a Trust with a Professional Corporation

Licensed professionals have a specific reason for establishing a revocable living trust and naming themselves as grantors and sole trustees. Doctors, dentists, lawyers, accountants, and other professionals who own their own professional corporations can set up their trusts to satisfy all legal requirements and still avoid probate in the event of their deaths.

The stock in a professional corporation must be owned by the individual with the professional license, for example, the doctor, the lawyer, or the orthodontist.

The law makes an allowance for the "professional corporation trust" to hold the stock owned by the licensed professional in the professional corporation. The professional corporation trust is simply a revocable living trust with a specific purpose: to keep a licensed individual's interest in a professional corporation out of probate in the event of the death of its owner.

This type of trust has certain restrictions. The successor trustee may administer the trust to sell its asset—the stock in the professional corporation—but not to practice the specific profession (e.g., medicine, law, accounting, or dentistry).

With this planning, a business won't be subject to a dramatic loss in value upon the death of the professional. Should the grantor meet an untimely demise, a successor trustee can have the authority to immediately liquidate the corporate assets or sell the ongoing business. In this way, the professional practice won't be too badly disrupted—as it most certainly would be if the practice had to go through probate. The monetary value of the practice can remain basically intact.

Another true story may offer the best explanation. An orthodontist established a revocable living trust and named a successor trustee. As it happened, this planning was of great benefit to his family. When he died unexpectedly of a heart attack, his wife became trustee of the stock in his professional corporation.

As anticipated in the trust, she was able to sell the ongoing practice to another practicing doctor within two weeks after her husband's death. If the orthodontist's practice had gone into probate, the practice could have quickly lost half its value—or more—for one simple reason: If the orthodontist isn't there when the patients need their braces adjusted, the patients, out of necessity, will take their business elsewhere.

One of my close friends, also a doctor, came by for a visit a few years ago. This was not unusual, as we often visited about various things, from business and taxes, religion and faith, to families and even death.

This time my friend seemed unusually concerned. He had had a distinct impression that he needed to have more life insurance to protect his family in the event that he should die. He had taken out several policies for millions of dollars and was now concerned that it would be a part of his taxable estate if he should indeed die.

After some consideration, I advised the good doctor that he should transfer ownership of his insurance to a family limited partnership. He should include his grown children in this partnership and restrict his rights to benefit from the insurance proceeds. With some planning and after full discussion with the family, a partnership was created and the insurance was transferred.

By being owned by the partnership, the insurance would not be a part of the doctor's taxable estate. It would not be subject to the three-year transfer rule to pull it back into his estate. And the family could still enjoy the benefits of the whole policy in the event of his death.

The doctor also reviewed his professional corporation to make sure it was protected by a professional corporation trust. He also updated his living wills and power of attorney.

Wouldn't you know that this doctor's actions were indeed brought about by a real premonition. The doctor decided on a complete physical. His brain was found to contain a rapidly growing cancerous tumor. He was dead within a year.

The spouse and family were grief stricken. But they were gratified that together the doctor and I had protected his estate and his insurance. The widow and the children had vigorous hugs for me at the subsequent meetings for legal reviews.

Sadly, not all professionals allow themselves to take such counsel to heart. I still have regular discussions with my dentist (not while he is drilling on my teeth) about how he should protect his business and his estate for his family. He is convinced that he doesn't even have enough in his estate to worry about it. He has five children (mostly grown), a spouse, a beautiful house, and drives a new Nissan 300 ZX. If you were his family, do you think he should worry about it?

///

Action Items—Chapter 13: Something for Doctors to Consider

As a physician or dentist you may have a even greater need to structure your business and personal finances in a way that not only optimizes your tax breaks but also provides protection of your family's assets from business liabilities and vice versa. To help you better visualize the examples given in this chapter I have prepared a sample of those provided to my clients.

Go to *www.EstatePlanningDr.com/book* to download:

Estate Planning & Entity Flow Chart

///

Chapter Fourteen

Special Suggestions
for Multi-level Marketers

There are some great privately owned business in the nation. One of the types of business that attracts people who are gregarious, out-going, and creative is referred to as the multi-level marketing phenomenon. You have surely been contacted at sometime in your life by someone from Arbonne International, Mannetech Associates, Amway, or even FreeLife-the Himalayan Goji Company. I have been contacted by representatives from each of them and more. These are multi-level marketing companies.

When you become successful in any one of these companies you have your own individually owned business. Most of these companies, if not all of them, recommend that you conduct your business through some type of business entity—a corporation, a partnership, or a limited liability company—and most successful business owners do. Such companies promote the business and tax benefits of having your own business entity.

You or your company will become an independent marketing associate of the parent company. You receive your compensation through your company. And your compensation will grow according to the number of associates you successfully convince to also market these products in their "downline." You make money not only by selling products but also by signing up other marketers to market under your line. Your business can become a very successful business. And while building your business, you receive training in sales techniques, in increasing your own self-esteem, and in business techniques.

Each of these businesses teaches its associates that the business they build can be passed on to their families or heirs under their will or trust. That language to do so is included in the parent company's associate agreement so the associates all know, or should know, that they should do some planning to protect their business from a death or incapacity. Unfortunately, many of these same associates never get around to the planning. It's something to do later. "Right now I'm working on my business!"

Naturally, working on the business, meeting new friends, attending sales conventions, and other stimulating activities, are much more exciting than planning for your eventual demise. But such planning is nevertheless important. No one knows how long they will live. And Death comes unexpectedly!

This is on my mind because I am working with a young lady at the present time who has been very successful in creating an independent Arbonne International multi-level marketing business of her own. She sells lots of product. She has independent associates working for her in her "down-line." She lives in a lavish home, has stylish clothing, drives impressive automobiles, and has a young family. She presents a wonderful image.

Unfortunately, she hasn't felt too vigorous lately and visited her doctor not long ago. As her doctor explained some medical tests she had recently taken at his request, he had to advise her that she has an un-treatable disease. He expects that she has only about 6 months left to live.

Of course, she was devastated. But she is determined to try to conquer her disease. In the meantime, she is making sure that her successful business will pass to her heirs without interruption. I feel sorry for her situation. But I commend her for her actions. This planning we are now just bringing to completion will allow her business to continue. Her children will be provided for. And her taxes will be reduced.

How great would it be if all those who enter into a business associate agreement with any multi-level marketing company would take a moment to consider what would happen to their business if they for some reason were suddenly not there. Who would take over? How would it happen? How expensive and time consuming would it be? And above all, what can they do to make sure things go the way they intend!

///

Action Items—Chapter 14: Special Suggestions for Multi-level Marketers

If you are an independent distributor owning your own business with a multi-level marketing company, you may be able to will your business and residual income to your heirs. This is wonderful! Even so, you may not have yet taken the time to review the details of how that will come to pass. Are you familiar with the specific details on how that may be handled? Have you identified those *who* would take over and *what* they will need to do? Are there any *costs* involved? Knowing these answers will assist you in structuring your business and estate in a way that can ensure a smooth transition without unnecessary delays and expenses.

Go to *www.EstatePlanningDr.com/book* to download:

Willable Residual Income-Analysis Form

///

Chapter Fifteen

Your Estate Planning Action List

Now that you're reading about estate planning, keep up the momentum! Follow the
steps in this chapter to create a comprehensive estate plan
to provide for your family. Keep in mind that your revocable living trust will be the foundation of your estate
plan. It will provide you with protection for your personal
and business assets. It will give you more than peace of
mind—you'll avoid probate and efficiently, quickly, and
inexpensively pass your estate on to your heirs.

As a reminder, a revocable living trust provides these
benefits:
- Helps you avoid paying excess taxes
- Addresses the issue of your becoming mentally
  or physically incapacitated (the most neglected
  problem in estate planning)
- Helps you select the best type of power of attorney
- Helps you face the reality of the importance of a
  living will

- Addresses the issue that, legally, a minor child is considered an incapacitated person
- Allows professionals who hold stock in their own corporation to protect the corporation from serious loss of value in the event of that person's death
- Solves the problems inherent in joint tenancy, right of survivorship, and community property

Use this chapter as a checklist to take the next step: take charge of your estate plan!

Step 1: List Your Assets and Collect Important Papers

As you list your assets, be sure to assign an actual or estimated value to each asset.

- Create or update your list of assets such as your home, other real estate, automobiles, stocks, bonds, cash, or business property. This is the basis for the schedule of trust assets you'll compile with your estate planning attorney.
- Compile your important records including your current will if you have one, property titles, automobile titles, investment summaries, etc.
- Create or update your personal property list. Include antiques, collectibles, coin collections, works of art, furniture, jewelry, and heirlooms. Take this list to your estate planning attorney to review. Remember, you'll keep this list at home and be able to update it regularly.

Step 2: Estimate the Value of Your Assets

The total estimated value of your assets may surprise you. Most people discover they're worth more than they thought. Refer to the figure below to determine if your estate is large enough to be subject to estate taxes upon your death.

For the year:	The Applicable Exclusion Amount for U.S. Federal Estate Taxes
2000 and 2001	$675,000
2002 and 2003	$1 million
2004 and 2005	$1.5 million
2006 to 2008	$2 million
2009	$3.5 million
2010	N/A (estate taxes repealed!)
2011	$1 million (watch for changes by Congress!)

Figure 13.1—The applicable exclusion rate for United States federal estate taxes. If you die in the year 2007, for example, your estate is exempt from federal estate taxes if it's valued at less than $2 million.

Step 3: Determine Your Objectives

Determine your objectives for planning your estate and write them down. Use the following questions to help you think about your goals and wishes:

- What do you want to happen in the event of your death?

- Do you want everything to go to your spouse? To your children? To your church or favorite charity?
- Would you like to avoid probate?
- Do you want to eliminate any publicity regarding the settlement of your estate?
- Would you like to reduce the costs to settle the estate?
- Do you want to reduce the taxes?
- Should you provide for your protection in the event of your incapacity?
- Do you have other objectives you want to accomplish?

Step 4: Address Important Issues

Sit down with your spouse, adult child, or other family member and make important decisions regarding these critical issues:

- Choose your personal representative for your will and your successor trustee for your revocable living trust. Remember, this doesn't have to be your attorney.
- If your children are minors, who will care for them? Consider your options, select a friend or relative to be their guardian, ask that person, and then plan to include this designation in your new revocable living trust.
- Decide if want your heirs to receive their full inheritance upon your death. Would you rather

provide for them in a stair-stepped manner? If so, plan to include these instructions in your new trust.
- Discuss living wills. Clearly discuss your wishes for various scenarios. For more information on living wills, refer to *www.PocketLivingWill.com.* Your attorney should prepare a living will for you as part of the revocable living trust package.

Step 5: Find an Experienced Estate Planning Lawyer

It's imperative that you find an attorney who specializes in estate planning and has experience creating revocable living trusts. When calling attorneys, ask these questions:
- What is your area of specialty?
- Have you drafted revocable living trusts?
- To create a trust, will I counsel directly with an attorney or will I be talking with the office paralegal?
- What do your fees include? Please give me specifics.
- What kind of service can I expect? Can I call and ask questions if problems arise? Does your office charge for the phone call?
- How much does it cost to create an estate plan with a revocable living trust? How do you determine your fees? And what does your fee include?
- How do you determine your fee to settle an estate? How much do you typically charge to settle an estate with a revocable living trust?

Step 6: Create Your Estate Planning Package

Work with your estate planning attorney to create a complete estate plan. Your basic estate plan should include the following:

1. Living trust document (with A/B trust election for a married couple, if needed)
2. Backup pour-over will
3. Schedule of trust assets
4. Assignment of personal property
5. Deeds to transfer real estate (including your residence)
6. Documents for the transfer of assets to your revocable living trust
7. Guidelines for trustee
8. Letter to successor trustee
9. Instructions on how to keep your trust current
10. General durable power of attorney
11. Living will and medical power of attorney
12. Glossary of legal terms
13. Notary and witness service
14. A trust binder and organizer

An Urgent Call to Action

Don't wait another day to plan your estate. I urge you to take time to address these steps and contact an experienced attorney who specializes in estate planning right away. It's critical that you put your affairs in order, set up a revocable living trust, and ensure your heirs receive their inheritance in a manner that exactly follows your wishes. Start today!

Action Items—Chapter 15: Your Estate Planning Action List

I would like to invite you to review the Confidential Estate Planning Questionnaire I have created that will help you gather the proper information to create your estate plan. Get one at *www.EstatePlanningDr.com/book*

Then contact my office to complete your planning:

Steven W. Allen, P.C.
1550 E. McKellips Rd. Suite 111
Mesa, AZ 85203
(480) 644-0070 | FAX (480) 644-0072
Steve@EstatePlanningDr.com

Quick Order Form

Book Title	Quantity	Price
Action Guide —You Can't Take It With You ... So How Will You Leave It Behind? Workbook with 3 Audio CDs and 2 Talking PowerPoint Presentations $197.00		
You Can't Take It With You ... So How Will You Leave It Behind? ISBN: 978-1-879033-97-9 hardcover $27.95		
The Illegal Trial of Christ ISBN: 978-1-879033-31-3 hardcover $19.95		
Founding Fathers: Uncommon Heroes ISBN: 978-1-879033-76-4 softcover $19.95		
Founding Fathers: Uncommon Heroes on CD ISBN: 978-1-879033-75-7 audio book on 6 CDs $24.95		
Give Me Liberty ISBN: 978-1-879033-12-2 hardcover $12.95		
Pocket Living Will Credit-card size living will to carry with you $27.00		
Shipping		
Total		

Fax: 1-480-644-0072. Send this form.
Postal Orders: Legal Awareness Series, LLC
Call: Toll-Free: 1-800-733-5297
1550 E. McKellips Rd. #111
Mesa, AZ 85203
Online: secured ordering at *http://www.legalawareness.com*

Shipping:
USA: $8.00 for first item; add $2.00 for each additional item
AZ residents please include 8.1% tax

Please Print:

Name _____

Company _____

Ship To _____

City/State/Zip _____

Phone _____ E-mail Address _____

Credit card # _____ Expires: _____

Name on Card _____

Billing Address _____

❑ Visa   ❑ Master Card   ❑ American Express

Please sign _____

To book Steven W. Allen to speak at your conference or event call
1-800-733-5297 or e-mail **Steve@EstatePlanningDr.com**

Index

A/B trusts, 69–70, 98–99, 165–166
Action list for estate planning, 247–253
Affidavit of the Notice to Creditors, 35
Affidavit of the Notice to the Heirs
  and Beneficiaries, 35
Applicable exclusion amounts, 66–67,
  98, 165–166
Asset protection trusts, 188–190
Attorney-prepared wills, 23–25, 28–29
Attorneys
  Choosing, 124, 140–150, 251
  Fees with probate, 40–41
  Named as personal
    representatives, 112–114

Bonds, executor of estate and, 24
Business planning, 203–204
  Linking businesses to estate plan,
    231–236
  Business deductions and,
    219–230
  Sole proprietorships, 204–206
  General proprietorships,
    206–207
  C-corporations, 208–210
  Subchapter-S corporations,
    210–211, 214

Limited liability corporations,
  211–212, 215–216, 232
Selecting a business entity,
  213–216

Capital gains taxes
  Sale of residence, 188
  Charitable remainder trusts
    and, 181
C-corporations, 208–210
Charging orders, family limited
  partnerships and, 158–161
Charitable remainder trusts, 178–187
Charitable remainderem, 180
Children
  Considered legally incapacitated,
    80–83
  Guardianship of, 21, 81, 82–83,
    100, 250
  Revocable living trusts and,
    80–83
Community property, 85–88, 100,
  175–178
Conservatorship, 119
  Revocable living trusts and, 73
Co-settlors, 47–48
Co-trustees, 47–48

Covey, Steven R., 129
Creditors. *See* Liability.
Crummy powers, 171–173

Death benefits, 163–166, 168, 171–174
Debts. *See* Liability.
Deductions, business, 205, 213, 215, 219–228
Discounted value, in family limited partnerships, 157
Distributions from estates, 111–112
Durable power of attorney, 77

Estate recovery, 197
Estate taxes
 Applicable exclusion amounts, 66–67
 Avoiding probate through revocable living trusts, 117–118
 Irrevocable life insurance trusts, 163–166, 168–173, 174–175
 Life insurance and, 108
 Liquid asset protection plans and, 190–193
 Revocable living trusts and, 66–70, 117–118
 Wills and, 106–108
Estate value
 Probate and, 33
 State minimums and, 33
Estates, defined, 19
Executor of estate, defined, 24

Family limited partnerships, 151–163
 Asset protection trusts and, 189
 Charging orders and, 158–161
 Discounted value in, 157
 Gifts and, 155
 K-1 tax reports and, 159
 Taxes and, 108, 155, 157, 160–163

Fiduciary duty, 119

General proprietorships, 206–207
Gift taxes, 164, 169–172, 177
Gifts
 Personal residence trusts and, 187–188
 Charitable organizations, 185–187
 Tax implications of, 155, 186
 Irrevocable life insurance trusts and, 164, 169–172, 174–175, 177, 178
Grantor retained income trusts, 187–188
Grantor trusts. *See* Living trusts.
Grantors, 46
Guardianship of children, 21, 81, 82–83, 100, 250

HIPAA language, 75, 77, 101–102
Holographic wills, 22–23
Home-based businesses, 220–224
Homes. *See* Property.

Incapacitation
 C-corporations and, 209–210
 General proprietorships and, 207
 Limited liability corporations and, 212
 Minor children and, 80–83
 Revocable living trusts and, 70–78
 Sole proprietorships and, 205–206
 Subchapter-S corporations and, 211
 Trustees and, 119–120
Income beneficiaries
 Charitable remainder trusts and, 179–180

Income taxes
  Family limited partnerships
    and, 160–163
  Sole proprietorships and, 205
Incorporation, 214–215
Insurance
  Life insurance, 108, 163–174
  Malpractice insurance, 237–238
  Taxes on insurance proceeds, 108
  See also Charitable remainder
    trusts, Irrevocable life
    insurance trusts.
Inter vivos trusts. See Living trusts.
Intestate wills, 20–22
Inventory and Appraisement, 36–37
Irrevocable life insurance trusts
  As beneficiary, 174
  Charitable remainder trusts
    and, 182–183
  Community property states
    and, 175–178
  Estate taxes and, 163–166,
    168–173, 174–175
  Gifts and, 164, 169–172, 174–175,
    177, 178
Irrevocable trusts, defined, 45

Joint tenancy
  Probate and, 113
  With right of survivorship,
    85–98, 100

K-1 tax reports, 159

Last will and testament, 26, 96,
  121–122
Lawsuits. *See* Liability.
Lawyers
  Choosing, 124, 140–150, 251

Fees with probate, 40–41
Named as personal
  representatives, 112–114
Letters Testamentary, 34–35
Liability
  C-corporations and, 208, 209
  Family limited partnerships,
    protection against, 158–162
  General proprietorships and, 207
  Limited liability corporations
    and, 212
  Liquidating property to pay
    debt, 111
  Protection for the non-wealthy,
    195–196
  Sole proprietorships and, 205
  Subchapter-S corporations
    and, 211
Licensed professionals, planning
  for, 237–242
Life insurance
  Estate taxes and, 108
  Estate value and, 108
  Irrevocable life insurance trusts,
    163–174
  Death benefits of, 163–166, 168,
    171–174
  See also Irrevocable life insurance
    trusts
Limited liability corporations,
  211–212, 215–216, 232
Limited partnerships, 232
Liquid asset protection plans,
  190–193
Living probate, 71
Living trusts
  A/B trust elections and, 98–99
  Accountability to beneficiaries,
    120

Benefits of, 247–248
Business entities linked to, 231–236
Business tax deductions and, 224–225
Children and, 80–83
Community property and, 85–88
Complete, 98–101
Conservatorship and, 73
Contesting, 109
Cost of, 111, 122, 124–125
Defined, 45
Estate taxes and, 66–70, 106–108, 117–118
Examples of use, 131–137
Incapacitation, physical or mental, 70–78, 119–120
Items left out of, 116–117
Joint tenancy with right of survivorship and, 85–98
Living wills and, 78–80
Loans with property in, 123–124
Personal representatives and, 112–114
Pour-over wills and, 121–122
Power of attorney in, 74–78
Privacy and, 106
Professional corporations used with, 83–85, 238–241
Property in more than one state, 105–106
Schedule of trust property and, 123
Setting up, 139–150
Stock owned by business owner and, 214
Subchapter-S corporation stock held in, 210
Successor trustees and, 118–119

Trustees of, 119–120, 122
Validity among states, 110, 114
Living wills, 78–80, 100–101

Malpractice insurance, 237–238
Marital deduction trusts. *See* A/B trusts.
Medicaid
Planning for, 196–199
Medicaid annuities, 199–201
Medicaid annuities, 199–201
Medical power of attorney, 100–101
Minor children
Considered legally incapacitated, 80–83
Guardianship of, 21, 81, 82–83, 100, 250
Multi-level marketers, considerations for, 243–246

Noncountable assets, 199
Notice of Contribution, 171

Personal property lists, 27–29
Personal residence trusts, 187–188
Personal representatives
Attorneys named as, 112–114
Power to liquidate property, 111–112
Petition for Admission to probate, defined, 34
Power of attorney
Durable power of attorney, 77
Medical, 100–101
Revocable living trusts and, 74–78
Springing, 77
Probate
Affidavit of the Notice to Creditors and, 35

Affidavit of the Notice to the
Heirs and Beneficiaries and, 35
Attorneys' fees with, 40–41
Community property and, 85,
87–88
Confidentiality and, 39
Cost of, 39–41, 103–104, 110–111,
124
Defined, 31
Estate planning and, 41–42
Examples of process, 33–37
Exceptions of, 32–33
Inventory and Appraisement
and, 36–37
Joint tenancy with right of
survivorship, 85–98
Length of process, 37–38
Letters Testamentary and, 34–35
Living probate, 71
Petition for Admission to
probate, defined, 34
Property in more than one state
and, 105–106
Questions concerning, 41–42
Rules of, 38
Steps of, 38
Stock owned by business
owner, 214
Time to complete process, 106
Trusts and, 43
Value of estate and, 33
Wills as public record in, 106
Procrastination on estate planning,
125–129
Professional corporation trusts,
83–85, 239
Professional corporations as successor
trustees, 120

Property
Community property, 85–88, 100
Joint tenancy with right of
survivorship, 85–98, 100
Liquidating to make
distributions, 111–112
Owned in more than one state,
60–61, 105–106
Owned through joint tenancy,
113
Pour-over wills and, 121–122
Testamentary trusts and, 105
Titled, 117
Pour-over wills, 96, 121–122

Real estate. *See* Property.
Relatives, nearest living
Intestate wills and, 20–22
Release of Community Property
document, 177
Revocable living trusts
A/B trust elections and, 98–99
Accountability to beneficiaries,
120
Benefits of, 247–248
Business entities linked to,
231–236
Business tax deductions and,
224–225
Children and, 80–83
Community property and, 85–88
Complete, 98–101
Conservatorship and, 73
Contesting, 109
Cost of, 111, 122, 124–125
Defined, 45
Estate taxes and, 66–70, 106–108,
117–118

Examples of use, 131–137
Incapacitation, physical or
   mental, 70–78, 119–120
Irrevocable trusts vs., 45
Items left out of, 116–117
Joint tenancy with right of
   survivorship and, 85–98
Living wills and, 78–80
Loans with property in, 123–124
Personal representatives and,
   112–114
Pour-over wills and, 121–122
Power of attorney in, 74–78
Privacy and, 106
Professional corporations used
   with, 83–85, 238–241
Property in more than one state,
   105–106
Schedule of trust property
   and, 123
Setting up, 139–150
Stock owned by business owner
   and, 214
Subchapter-S corporation stock
   held in, 210
Successor trustees and, 118–119
Successor trusts and, 122
Trustees of, 119–120, 122
Validity among states, 110, 114
Schedule of trust property, 123
Schiavo, Terri, 79
Self-employment taxes, 213–214, 216
Self-proving clause, 26–27
Self-proving wills, 27
Settlors, 46
Small business corporations. *See*
   Subchapter-S corporations.
Sole proprietorships, 204–206
Split-interest trusts, 186–187

Springing power of attorney, 77
Stocks
   Probate and, 214
   Revocable living trusts and, 84
Straw-man transfers, 87
Subchapter-S corporations, 210–211,
   214
Successor trustees, 48, 73–75, 118–119
   Professional corporations as, 120
Successor trusts, 122

Taxes
   Business deductions, 205, 213,
     215, 219–228
   Capital gains, 181, 188
   C-corporations and, 208–209
   Choosing business entity, 213
   Estate taxes, 66–70, 106–108,
     163–166, 168–173, 174–175,
     190–193
   Family limited partnerships and,
     108, 155–157, 160–163
   General partnerships and,
     206–207
   Gifts and, 155, 186
   Gift taxes, 164, 169–172, 177
   Income taxes, 160–163
   Limited liability corporations
     and, 212, 216
   Liquid asset protection plans
     and, 190–193
   Self-employment taxes, 213–214,
     216
   Sole proprietorships and, 205
   Subchapter-S corporations
     and, 211
Testamentary trusts, 24–25, 104–105
Trustees
   Co-trustees, 47–48

Incapacitation of, 119–120
Naming of, 119–120
Of irrevocable life insurance
   trusts, 172–174
Of revocable living trusts, 122
Successor, 48, 73–75, 119–120
Trustors, 46
Trusts
   A/B trusts, 69–70, 98–99,
      165–166
   Accountability to beneficiaries,
      120
   Asset protection trusts, 188–190
   Beneficiaries of, 46
   Charitable remainder trusts,
      178–187
   Children and, 80–83
   Community property and, 85–88
   Contesting, 109
   Defined, 43
   Estate taxes and, 66–70
   Grantor retained income trusts,
      187–188
   Incapacitation, physical or
      mental, 70–78, 119–120
   Irrevocable life insurance trusts,
      108, 163–178, 182–183
   Joint tenancy with right of
      survivorship and, 85–98
   Living wills and, 78–80
   Personal representatives and,
      112–114
   Personal residence trusts,
      187–188
   Power of attorney in, 74–78
   Probate and, 43
   Professional corporation trusts,
      83–85

Professional corporations used
   with, 83–85, 238–241
Requirements for, 46
Revocable living trusts. See
   separate entry.
Split-interest trusts, 186–187
Successor trustees and, 118–119
Testamentary trusts, 24–25,
   104–105
Trustees of, 119–120, 122
Validity among states, 110, 114

Unlimited marital deductions, 67–68

Wealth replacement insurance trust.
   See Charitable remainder trust.
Wills
   Attorney-prepared, 23–25, 28–29
   Attorneys as personal
      representatives, 112–113
   Contesting, 108–109
   Costs of creating, 113–114
   Costs of settling, 110–111
   Distributions from estate,
      111–112
   Estate taxes and, 106–108
   Holographic, 22–23
   Importance of, 19–20
   Intestate, 20–22
   Joint tenancy and, 113
   Last will and testament, 26, 96,
      121–122
   Letters Testamentary and, 35
   Living wills, 78–80
   Misconceptions about, 31–43,
      103–104
   Petition for Admission to
      Probate and, 34

Personal property lists and,
27–29
Personal representatives and,
112–114
Pour-over, 96, 121–122
Probate and, 31–33, 35, 106
Public record, matter of, 106
Reviewing, 41–42
Self-proving clause, 26–27
Self-proving wills, 27
Testamentary trusts, 104–105
Time required to probate, 106
Validity among states, 109–110,
114
Well-written, 25
Will Analysis form, 42
Witnesses
Holographic wills and, 22–23
Self-proving clause and, 26–27